# Handbook on Athletic Perfection

by

Wes Neal

Handbook on Athletic Perfection

Wes Neal

ISBN 978-1-938254-54-3

Cross Training Publishing
15418 Weir Street #177
Omaha, NE 68136
(308) 293-3891

www.crosstrainingpublishing.com



This book is manufactured in the United States of America.

Library of Congress Cataloging in Publication Data in Progress.

**To Peggy**

My best friend, honey and wife. Without your understanding, encouragement and commitment to this project it could never have been completed. Thanks, Pegs, I love you!


## SPECIAL ACKNOWLEDGEMENTS

Special appreciation is extended to the following persons for their contribution in the production of this book:

Bruce Day, Dan'l Hollis, Caria Hollis, Bruce Lester, Peggy Neal, Rodger Williams, Sandy Swan, Marty Mayer, Mike McCoy, Russ McKnight, Rod Sherman, Watson Spoelstra, John Werhas, Hazel Neal, Abe Getty, and Steve Strickland.

For Additional information on
Christian athletic publications:

www.crosstrainingpublishing.com

## A GLIMPSE OF JESUS CHRIST

Jesus came from Nazareth, a poorly thought of village in Galilee. A carpenter by trade, He knew what hard work, slivers in His hands and sweat were all about. He knew poverty and oppression first-hand. He constantly experienced prejudice; He was Jewish in a Roman governed community. When He taught, though He had no formal education, even those who did not agree with Him said He taught with authority.

He gave sight to the blind, healed lepers, walked on water, and raised the dead. Those who really knew Him claimed His greatest work was that He changed them into new men.

He made many thought provoking statements about Himself: "I am the way, and the truth, and the life; no one comes to the Father, but through Me . . . I and the Father are one . . . I came that they might have life, and might have it abundantly" (John 14:6, 10:30 and 10:10).

There were those who didn't agree with Him, mainly the religious leaders. They trumped up charges against Him, spit on Him, ripped the skin off His back, beat His face beyond recognition and then nailed Him to a cross. As He hung on the cross, with shoulders dislocated, He felt the pain of spikes in His wrists and feet.

At noon, total darkness came over the land. At 3 PM He was separated from His Father in payment for our rebellion against God. He died! His enemies thought that they were finally rid of Him—but on the third day after His death, He rose. Later, He appeared to more than five hundred people at one time! He ascended into heaven. He said that He would return!

# ABOUT THE AUTHOR

Wes Neal has been consulting with sport coaches and business leaders for over thirty years. He is considered the pioneer in implementing biblical principles into the competitive sports world, all based on the life and teachings of Jesus. He has also written Coaching Sports God's Way for the athlete. He is a seminary graduate, was the field director for Athletes in Action, a ministry of Campus Crusade for Christ, is a featured speaker for the Fellowship of Christian Athletes, and taught for 12 years at Kanakuk Kamp in Branson, Missouri. He currently lives with his wife, Peggy, in central Ohio. They have two grown daughters, and six grandchildren.

## TABLE OF CONTENTS

# INTRODUCTION

What you are about to read in this handbook is a new approach to athletic competition. Yet, the principles are as old as the Bible. In this handbook I've taken God's "tried and true" biblical principles and related them to the athlete of today.

Many people have asked how this handbook came about. As I relate to you its story, my hope is that you will become as excited as I am about its possible effect on your athletic performance. It's my desire for Jesus Christ to become the center of your athletic life. It's also my desire that as you learn to fellowship with Jesus during your athletic performance, you will experience a deeper walk with Him in all other areas of your life.

This handbook actually began a few years ago. While I was traveling the country with an evangelistic weightlifting team, I began to wonder if God had something to say about how an athlete could reach his maximum athletic potential. There were biblical principles for reaching one's maximum potential in other areas of life, such as one's family life. It seemed that God's Word would have something to say about an athlete reaching his fullest athletic potential.

A puzzling question to me was, "How do I lift weights the way God wants me to lift them?" I had no answer. I knew how to train to develop greater strength, but I didn't know for certain that I was doing it God's way.

A close friend and weightlifting partner on the team, Dan Hollis, and I used to talk about this subject for hours at a time. Yet, neither of us could answer the question with any certainty. At the tour's end I began to research the Bible in search for an answer.

To my excitement, truths began to leap at me from the Bible. I wrote each passage that related to this question on a 3X5 card. Before I was through, my stack of cards was six inches high. Then, I sorted the cards into categories. Next, I began to apply these principles to my weightlifting workouts. Immediately, I noticed two results. First, my fellowship with God continued throughout my entire lifting session. That was a new experience for me. Those training hours, in the past, were always set apart from fellowship with God. Now, He was actually a part of my lifting. Secondly, I noticed a greater intensity in my workouts. I had greater motivation than ever before. And, it was consistent day after day! This greater intensity soon led to faster improvement. In fact, at a reduced body weight I actually lifted heavier weights.

I compiled this "new" information into manuscript form and wrote the book *The Handbook on Athletic Perfection.* Since then, I have had numerous opportunities to counsel athletes and coaches through the country on how to apply God's Word to the athletic performance. This new edition, *Handbook on Athletic Perfection,* contains most of the information in the former book and many new principles.

One of the questions coaches and athletes have asked is, "Why should a Christian place an emphasis on athletics?" Many gifted athletes quit sports because they cannot relate Christianity to athletic competition. I see four reasons for a Christian to pursue athletics if he has been given the talent to do so.

**1. A person is to remain in that same condition as he was in when he became a Christian.**

> "Brethren, let each man remain in that condition in which he was called."
>
> 1 Corinthians 7:24

This, of course, does not mean God cannot call you into a new area of activity. It only means that you just don't drop what you're doing when you become a Christian. If the Lord wants you in a new area of activity He will reveal that to you. Some of His ways of revealing something like this are His Word, counsel of others, circumstances and the peace only He can give.

**2. The talents you have been given are from God and are designed for a purpose.**

> "The Lord has made everything for its [His] own purpose . . ."
>
> Proverbs 16:4

You have a responsibility to invest those talents as wisely as you know how for whatever purpose God has designed them.

**3. An athlete has a built-in platform for sharing the good news of Jesus Christ.**

In America, athletics are a prime form of entertainment for thousands upon thousands of people. People listen to what an athlete says. They listen, not because he is an expert on the subject, but because they have a familiarity with him. They have either seen him in action or read about him. That platform can be used to share the good news of Jesus Christ.

**4. You will understand more clearly how to apply God's Word to your non-athletic world as you apply It to your athletic performance.**

One of the most important benefits of athletics is that it is a microcosm of life. Competitive athletics provide us with a mirror for our real attitudes. It's interesting that frequently the same attitudes we show in athletics are those we show in non-athletic activities when situations are similar. For instance, picture a golfer dribbling the ball off a tee after having taken a mighty swing. He gets so upset with himself that he takes his driver and breaks it in two.

That same temper flare-up is also seen when he receives a bill in the mail.

He expected the bill, but there is an added charge he didn't expect. He reacts the same as he did when things didn't go his way on the golfing tee. He rips the bill in two in another temper flare-up.

As you apply God's Word to your athletic performance, you will understand more clearly how to apply it to other areas of your life.

This handbook is designed to help you understand how God's Word does apply to your athletic performance. You won't necessarily become a better athlete by diligently applying the concepts in this handbook. But, you will develop into the maximum athlete God has designed you to be.

Most likely, that will be great improvement! You cannot expect the highest results by just reading this handbook and setting it aside. It must be studied, applied, discussed and studied some more. However, it is only a handbook. The Bible is the only ultimate source of information on God's way of doing things.

In the chapters of this handbook, you will come to grips with the word "perfect" over and over again. Our natural tendency is to think that no one can be perfect.

But you can be perfect in your athletic performance. Let's go to the first chapter and see how!

Wes Neal

# HOW TO STUDY THIS HANDBOOK

The following suggestions are to help you apply the concepts of this handbook to your athletic performance in the most effective way.

1. Read through the entire handbook to get an overall picture of how it ties together.

Each chapter works with the other to form the complete picture. This overview will help you understand each individual chapter better.

2. Study individual chapters making notes of what you can immediately apply to your athletic performance.

3. Discuss the questions at the end of each chapter with another athlete who is also studying the same chapter.

If no one is available be sure to answer the questions yourself.

4. Make application of each chapter in actual athletic competition.

This is what it's all about—you, the Lord and your athletic performance! For best results, spend at least one week on applying each chapter.

5. If you are training with another athlete using these concepts, discuss what you learn with each other after the workout.

Remember, it takes time to develop new attitudes. Because of this, the Perfect Athletic Performance will always take a conscious effort on your part.

## CHAPTER 1

# PERFECTION

Picture yourself as the perfect athlete. Your skills excel those of other athletes. Physical and mental errors are as out of place in your performance as a heat wave in a December snow storm. You are always in peak condition.

Routine execution for you is the perfect blend of maximum strength speed, coordination, reflex action, accuracy and timing. Your mind sends nerve impulses through your body for just the right touch in every situation You are an amazing athlete!

Statistics are not kept on you in baseball since you always get a hit and never make an error. You carry out every assignment in football with 12 on a 10 point scale. It is not a question, in basketball, of what kind of a percentage shooter you are since everything you put in the air goes in the basket. So it goes in every sport. You are the model of perfection in every sport's textbook.

This seems unrealistic, doesn't it? No athlete is like this. Imperfections are as common in athletics as sand on the seashore. Cicero, a Roman politician living in the century before the birth of Jesus Christ, put it this way, "Nothing is harder to find than perfection." His words might just as well have been written with the athlete in mind. Statistics reveal the imperfections existing in every athlete. Statistics show how far short from the world's standard of perfection an athlete performs.

Yet, one of the most penetrating statements of Jesus Christ is, "Therefore, you are to be PERFECT, as your heavenly Father is perfect" (Matthew 5:48). Notice that Jesus did not say that perfection is to be a far-off goal. He clearly said that you are to be perfect with the **same perfection** as God Himself. **An athlete can be perfect in everything he does.** Keep this in mind and you'll see how in this chapter.

Seldom do two people get the same picture in their mind when they hear a certain word. For instance, when someone says that they just bought a blue car, you picture a light blue car with a greenish tint. The actual color of his car is dark blue. So it is with the word **perfect.** One person interprets it as absolutely no room for improvement. Another person sees it as a pre-set standard, such as the 300 batting average in baseball. In the context Jesus uses the word, in Matthew 5:48, there is no question about His application. Let's capture that scene in our minds.

Jesus made His statement to a huge crowd of people gathered around Him. Skeptics were there among those who accepted everything He said as truth. Most of His listeners had one thing in common. They believed they would gain God's approval if they kept the many religious regulations handed down by the religious leaders. It's the same as saying you have God's approval by achieving the world's standard of perfection (e.g., a 300 batting average in baseball, a 100 yard rushing average in football or a 20 point average in basketball). Jesus set the record straight!

Jesus set the stage with five challenging statements. Each statement began with, "You have heard that it was said . . ." or "You have heard that the ancients were told . . ." He then accurately stated a standard of perfection commonly accepted by His listeners which He followed with an authoritative, "But I say to you . . ." **Jesus contrasted man's way with God's way. He contrasted man's idea of perfection with God's idea of perfection.**

His first statement on the common standard of perfection was, "You shall not commit murder . . ." (Matthew 5:21). Possibly there were a few smug smiles since most of His listeners considered themselves approved by that standard. Jesus continued, "But I say to you that everyone who is angry with his brother shall be guilty before the court . . ." (Matthew 5:22).

Uh oh! He burst the bubble of their self-righteousness wide open. Who among them had not been angry at one time or another? Then came the issue of morality. He said, "You have heard that it was said, 'You shall not commit adultery . . .' " (Matthew 5:27). Now in a crowd so large, there could have been some people guilty of this. But, more than likely, most of His listeners assumed He was talking to someone else. He added, "But I say to you, that everyone who looks on a woman to lust for her has committed adultery with her already in his heart" (Matthew 5:28). Wow! Jesus was sure on target bursting bubbles!

His intention was not simply to usher in a new ethical code. They already had books thick with rules and the right way to do things. He was deliberately contrasting two standards of perfection. The common standard of perfection was a legalistic carrying-out-the-letter of the law. It had nothing to do with one's attitudes as the letter of the law was carried out. **God's standard of perfection deals with our attitudes.** It is from these attitudes that our actions flow.

The same two standards of perfection are part of your athletic life. The "perfection" Jesus referred to in Matthew 5:48 is God's way for you to perform. It does not refer to sinless perfection. God will bring us to that state after our life on earth is over, not before. Jesus referred to a perfection of doing everything God's way as He is the standard for perfection.

It deals with your attitudes and has nothing to do with the degree of your mental and physical ability. God's way is not the world's way. He is far more interested in the character of a person than with statistics of his performance. Yet, God is vitally concerned with the development of your athletic skills. He gave them to you for a purpose. He desires them to be utilized for His perfect plan.

> "The Lord has made everything for its [His] own purpose, Even the wicked for the day of evil."
>
> (Proverbs 16:4)

When the world hangs a label of "perfect" on a performance, there are usually many factors that fall into place that could just as well have broken the performance. For instance, a perfect game for a baseball pitcher might be the result of some "lucky breaks." Several outs could have been made by sensational fielding plays. A perfect night at bat might have been made possible by the late start a fielder made in attempting to get to a routine fly ball. This is true in every sport. Athletic perfection, by the world's standard, has many factors. Some can be labeled "lucky breaks." But there are no "lucky breaks" in perfection from God's viewpoint. It is a matter of choice. The option must be exercised moment by moment if one is to perform God's way as it is revealed through the life and person of Jesus Christ. It is a conscious choice! **Unless you are consciously thinking God's thoughts, you are not thinking His thoughts.** The same is true concerning your actions. **Unless you are consciously performing His way, you are not performing His way.** Your actions are a product of what you think.

This is made clear for us in Isaiah 55:8–9:

> vs. 8 For My thoughts are **not** your thoughts,
> Neither are your ways My ways; declares the Lord.
> vs. 9 For as the heavens are higher than the earth,
> So are My ways higher than your ways,
> And My thoughts than your thoughts."

Our natural way of thinking and performing is not a reflection of God's thoughts and actions. It is not natural to love when I'm wronged. It is not natural for me to be patient in the midst of problems. This will be elaborated further in the chapter, "The Holy Spirit of Perfection."

The world's standard of athletic perfection is **external.** For the running back in football it might be a 100 yard average. For the tennis player it might be ten aces in a match. The golfer's standard of athletic perfection might be two putts on every green. For the world, outward results are more important than your attitudes and purpose. Yet God tells us, "All the ways of a man are clean in his own sight, but the Lord weighs the motives" (Proverbs 16:2).

Athletic perfection from God's viewpoint begins in the inside. It flows from your mind to outward results that can be seen in your actions. It is not a lazy attitude.

Jesus used the word "perfect" in Matthew 5:48 to describe someone who consciously chooses to think and perform God's way.

His attitudes reflect those of Jesus Christ. His actions honor God because they are an outpouring of His attitudes.

With this in mind, let's put a handle on athletic perfection.

> **ATHLETIC PERFECTION IS CONSCIOUSLY THINKING AND PERFORMING GOD'S WAY THROUGH THE EMPOWERMENT OF THE HOLY SPIRIT.**

Each athletic performance is an opportunity for you to think God's thoughts and perform His way. It's an opportunity for you to reflect His attitude in response to various circumstances. Your athletic performance will reflect the world's standard of perfection or God's standard of perfection.

God's standard of athletic perfection is not achieved by "lucky breaks." It is achieved by the **Christian athlete** who wants above everything else to please God. Here's the shocker. There is **nothing** you can do on your own power to think God's thoughts and perform His way. We're not talking about "do it God's way by your own boot straps." Remember the words of Isaiah 55:8, "For My thoughts are **not** your thoughts, neither are your ways My ways; declares the Lord."

We're talking about a performance pleasing to God because it is done His way and performed by His power. **The source of this power is Jesus Christ living through you by the Holy Spirit of God.** God's thoughts and ways are revealed to us in Jesus Christ.

> "No man has seen God at any time; the only begotten God (Son), who is the bosom of the Father, He has explained Him."
>
> (John 1:18)

Only through the work of the Holy Spirit can these thoughts and ways be brought to your consciousness. Jesus spoke of this to His disciples a short time before He was crucified.

> "These things I have spoken to you, while abiding with you. But the Helper, the Holy Spirit, whom the Father will send in My name, He will teach you all things, and bring to your remembrance all that I said to you."
> (John 14:25–26)

God's standard for athletic perfection can only be achieved if Jesus Christ is living in you through the Holy Spirit. How that happens will be detailed in the next three chapters. You are on the threshold of a great new athletic experience!

## FOR DISCUSSION

1. What difference is there between man's way and God's way in the athletic performance? How do these two different standards affect your performance?

2. To what degree have you been consciously thinking God's thoughts and performing His way in your athletic performance? Use current athletic performances to illustrate.

CHAPTER 2

# THE BEGINNING OF PERFECTION

The perfect athletic performance is one you do God's way. But, to do it God's way you need God's power. You can never experience it on your own power. God's power is available only in Jesus Christ. Because of a remarkable act of God, you are able to experience that power in your athletic performance. Here we will see how Jesus Christ can become your foundation for a perfect athletic performance.

Just for a moment let's focus attention on you. How would other people describe you? What would they say? "Great!" "Terrific!" "Nice!" "All right!" Those words don't say a lot, do they? People who know you could go into detail concerning your likes and dislikes. "He likes chocolate cake and football." "She likes volleyball and football players." That might describe you a little better. People who know you more intimately could disclose things that might even surprise you. But, who are you?

An anatomy student could describe you as a person with 206 bones, 639 muscles and a complex of 50,000 miles of blood vessels intertwining throughout your body. Your brain weighs approximately three pounds. Anatomy can tell interesting things about how you're made, but who are you, really?

Only the Bible explains who you are. You are the work of God. You are the masterpiece of all God's creation!

> "For Thou didst form my inward parts; Thou didst weave me in my mother's womb. I will give thanks to Thee, for I am fearfully and wonderfully made; Wonderful are Thy works, And my soul knows it very well. My frame was not hidden from Thee When I was made in secret And skillfully wrought in the depths of the earth. Thine eyes have seen my unformed substance; And in Thy book they were all written, The days that were ordained for me, When as yet there was not one of them."
>
> (Psalms 139:13–16)

You didn't just happen by chance. You were designed by the Architect of this world. Do you know how absurd it would be to think you just happened with no design from the Creator? Let's say you have a watch with many delicate mechanisms. If you took the watch completely apart, put the pieces in a paper sack, shook the sack and threw the pieces into the air, what chance do you think the watch would have to come back together again all by itself? It's about the same chance you would have to come together without the design and workmanship of God Himself. You are completely unique and have a dignity only God can give you.

> "When I consider Thy heavens, the work of Thy fingers,
> The moon and the stars, which Thou hast ordained;
> What is man, that Thou dost take thought of him?
> And the son of man, that Thou dost care for him?
> Yet Thou has made him a little lower than God (the angels),
> And dost crown him with glory and majesty!"
>
> (Psalms 8:3–5)

## YOUR PURPOSE

Unique as you are, it's impossible to understand your purpose for living without Jesus Christ. Your purpose is to have a continuing fellowship with God by bringing glory to Him, but there is no way this can be experienced on your own merit. The Bible explains it this way:

> ". . . for all have sinned and fall short of the glory of God . . ."
>
> (Romans 3:23)

## SIN DEFINED

The word "sin" is an archery term. It means "missing the mark." The "sin-mark" is that distance between the bull's-eye on a target and the actual place the arrow hits.

When the Bible tells us that we have sinned, it is describing our missing the mark of God's perfection. We fall short of His glory (the revealed greatness and grandeur of God). That creates a problem. There is no possible way to fellowship with God in that condition. Just as oil cannot mix with water, sin cannot mix with God. Fellowship means two or more people sharing things in common and participating together in these things. For instance, players on a ball team have fellowship by sharing a team name, coaches, equipment, etc. When these players share the same likes and dislikes, the bond of fellowship is even closer.

One of the most amazing runs in Rose Bowl history illustrates our break in fellowship with God. The 1929 Rose Bowl game was to determine the No. 1 team in the country. Undefeated and untied Georgia Tech was facing undefeated and once-tied University of California.

Disaster struck in the second quarter of a scoreless game. Stumpy Thomason, carrying the ball for Georgia Tech, fumbled when hit on his own 36 yard line. Roy Riegels of California grabbed the ball in mid-air and raced toward the goal line. However, just as he was about to be swarmed under by a host of Georgia Tech players, Riegels planted his right foot and reversed direction. He ran toward his own goal line with shouting California players trying desperately to stop him. One of his teammates finally caught up to him on his own twelve yard line. The momentum was too great. He finally got turned around only to have a pack of grateful Georgia Tech players bury him on the one yard line. The bewildered Roy Riegels was consoled by amazed, but sympathetic, teammates. California elected to punt on first down in an attempt to get out of the bizarre situation. It was ironic that Riegels, now playing center, snapped the ball to the player who had tried to turn him around. His kick was blocked and Georgia Tech was given a two-point safety. Those two points proved to be the margin of victory for Georgia Tech, 8–7.

Riegels later said, when explaining how he felt, that it was difficult for him to believe he had done something so wrong. What Roy Riegels did was viewed by everyone in the Rose Bowl. He made a mistake. We all make mistakes. His was more obvious because of the situation. Perhaps no one noticed the missed blocks or tackles by other players in the game. But they all saw No. 11 gallop the wrong way and lose the game.

Riegels' sense of direction was less than perfect. He didn't mean to run the wrong way. Imperfect actions are simply the actions of imperfect people. The entire human race has fallen short of God's perfection. Not one of us deserves to have close fellowship with Him. In our own way, we are guilty of running the wrong way in our thought life and actions—going the opposite direction from God's goal for us.

> "All of us like sheep have gone astray, Each of us has turned to his own way."
>
> (Isaiah 53:6)

Even people who compare favorably against other people fall short of God's perfection. Let's say that some athletes are about to attempt a long jump over a canyon. The first athlete runs to the edge and takes off with a mighty leap. He sails out about twenty-three feet and crashes to the canyon bottom. The next really puts some "juice" into it. He doesn't want to end up like the first. He has a great takeoff. In fact, he sails out over the twenty-seven foot mark. He feels good that he out-jumped the first athlete. But he also fell short of the other side. Both ended up at the bottom of the canyon.

Another jumper with rockets attached to his back also falls short. This is true in our personal lives. It doesn't matter how we compare to other people. On our own merit we fall short of God's perfection and cannot be in fellowship with Him. But God did something about our situation.

> "For God so loved the world, that He gave His only begotten Son, that whoever believes in Him should not perish, but have eternal life."
>
> (John 3:16)

## GOD HAS TAKEN ACTION

For us to have perfect fellowship with God, two things had to be done. We could not do these things for ourselves. First, we had to be shown who God is. It's impossible to fellowship with someone you don't even know. In Jesus Christ, God made Himself known to us!

> "No man has seen God at any time; the only begotten God [Son], who is in the bosom of the Father, He has explained Him."
>
> (John 1:18)

The second thing God accomplished through Jesus Christ was to make it possible for us to have fellowship with Him. But wait! We already said that imperfect man cannot have fellowship with a perfect God. The two don't mix. But God did something to change our condition in His sight. Let's say that you're a multi-millionaire and someone owes you fifty thousand dollars. He might be a very nice person but he still owes you the money. He has absolutely no way to pay you back. He wants to but he can't. He deserves to go to prison. Legally you would be right in sending him there. Out of your love for him you cancel his debt, and then give him fifty thousand dollars more for a new start. God didn't just cancel a debt when we missed the mark. He made it possible for our complete **nature to change** and a whole new life to begin!

> "Therefore, if any man is in Christ, he is a NEW creature; the old things passed away; behold, new things have come."
>
> (2 Corinthians 5:17)

Let's not dismiss this passage too quickly. We don't want to miss the mark of God's perfection, but it's our very nature. After Roy Riegels disastrous run he commented, "I thought I was doing right . . ." We can have the greatest desire to please God but our imperfect nature makes it impossible. Therefore our nature must be changed. But we can't change our own nature.

God did something for us in Jesus Christ making it possible to have fellowship with Him by giving us a completely new nature. It wold be great if you forgave someone a debt of fifty thousand dollars and gave him fifty thousand dollars more for a fresh start. It would be even greater if you made that person a member of your own family. He would have the same rights and privileges as other members of your family. He would bear your name. He would be your heir. That's exactly what God did for us in Jesus. Christ He made it possible for us to fellowship with Him now and throughout all eternity! How did He accomplish this? Before we could have this fellowship with God, a penalty had to be paid for our sin. The apostle Paul explained how this penalty has been paid for us.

> "For the wages [penalty] of sin is death [separation from God the Father], but the free gift of God is eternal life [never-ending fellowship with Him] in Jesus Christ our Lord."
>
> (Romans 6:23)

There is nothing we can do to pay our own penalty since we're all guilty of missing the mark. It could only be paid by someone not guilty. Even in our law system, one person sentenced to life imprisonment cannot serve a life sentence for someone else. They're both guilty and both must pay the penalty. Jesus Christ was innocent of missing the mark. Here's basically what happened.

1. Our natural end was death—eternal separation from God.

2. We are powerless to pay our own penalty and have fellowship with God.

3. Jesus Christ, who was perfect, paid our penalty for us.

> "He [God] made Him [Jesus Christ] who knew no sin to be sin on our behalf [take our place on the cross], that we might become the righteousness of God in Him [God sees the perfection of Jesus Christ in us]."
>
> (2 Corinthians 5:21)

4. This penalty payment is our free gift from God.

## THE GREATEST DECISION

God has provided the way to have fellowship with Him, but we must make the decision to take His way. We must personally accept a gift for it to be ours. The same is true of God's gift. We must personally accept it to make it our own. Jesus paid our penalty on the cross by representing us to His Father. The payment is ours when we accept it.

> "For God so loved the world, that He gave His only begotten Son, that whoever **believes** in Him should not perish, but have eternal life."
>
> (John 3:16)

The word "believe" is not an intellectual belief. It's a word used to describe what a person does when he accepts something as true and relies upon it as a way of life. One day a tightrope walker walked above a roaring waterfall. Hundreds gathered to watch his every step. Then he took a wheelbarrow across.

Again he received a tremendous ovation. He asked the audience if they believed he could safely wheel a man across the waterfall. "Sure we do" they replied.

He motioned a man down front to get in the wheelbarrow. That man left in a hurry!

He had an intellectual belief in the tightrope walker, but there was no way he was going to risk his life. When you have the John 3:16 kind of belief in Jesus, you are relying on Him with your life. He becomes your center core.

This kind of belief in Jesus Christ once was a new concept for me. Most of my life I thought I was a Christian. I went to church services and even served as an officer in a church youth group. I thought I was about as Christian as anyone could get when I enrolled in a theological seminary after college. But my life was no different than the lives of non-Christian friends. That disturbed me. I didn't experience any more power in my life than they did. I knew many facts about Jesus but I still didn't have a different quality in my life. One of the speakers at a conference I attended explained that it wasn't enough simply to know some facts about Jesus. He said that to become a Christian a person must willfully rely on Jesus Christ with his entire life. This was a practical reliance on Jesus. It included relying on the facts about Jesus in the Bible as well as relying on Him for life's goals, purpose and motivation. He explained that Christianity was a personal relationship with Jesus Christ. That's when I understood for the first time what it meant to believe in Jesus Christ.

I willfully decided to turn control of my life over to Jesus Christ and rely upon Him. I soon began to notice that I had a strong desire to learn more about Him. The close personal fellowship with God I had wanted became a reality.

Perhaps you have never understood what it means to believe in Jesus Christ. The decision you make to believe in Him is the most monumental you will ever make. You are acknowledging that He is the only way to have personal fellowship with God. You are acknowledging that Jesus Christ represented you on the cross and paid the penalty for your missing the mark of God's perfection. Finally, you are saying that you want Jesus Christ to take control of your life and replace your ambitions and goals with His. You want His thoughts to be your thoughts. You want His actions to be your actions. What happens when Jesus controls your life can be explained this way. You have basketball abilities that are inferior to those of another player.

You will never be able to duplicate his talent. You can copy his training program, follow his diet and wear his uniform, but you will never become him. Let's say that through some operation it was possible for him to enter your body.

Then you would experience the fullness of his abilities. He would be playing basketball through you.

So it is in the Christian experience. You can never copy the attitudes, thoughts and actions of Jesus Christ. When you believe in Him and accept Him, He lives His life through you.

It is your belief in Jesus Christ that makes you a Christian. The following prayer simply acknowledges that belief. The words are important only in that they represent your true desires. If they do, you can make this your prayer simply to express your inner belief in Jesus Christ.

> "Dear Father. Thank you for sending Jesus Christ to pay the penalty for my sin and for revealing Yourself to me through Him. I accept what You have done for me and commit myself to His control in my life."

The words of this prayer did not make you a Christian. Your belief in Jesus Christ did. Your relationship with God, established by your belief in Jesus Christ, **can never be broken!** You will always be in God's family throughout eternity. Jesus said, "My sheep hear My voice, and I know them, and they follow Me; and I give eternal life to them, and they **shall never perish;** and no one shall snatch them out of My hand" (John 10:27–28).

Since becoming a Christian I discovered that nobody can be a successful carbon copy of Jesus Christ. Imperfection can never copy perfection and get perfect results. The perfect athletic performance is Jesus Christ living and performing through you. If you believe in Him (totally rely upon Him), you have taken the first step in experiencing the perfect athletic performance. Next, we will view the role of the Holy Spirit in your perfect athletic performance.

## FOR DISCUSSION

1. What is our purpose as God's masterpiece of creation?
2. How does your tendency to do things your own way relate to God's definition of sin?
3. What two things must take place before we can have fellowship with God?
4. What has Christ done to make it possible for us to have fellowship with God?
5. How does one become a Christian?
6. What does it mean to "believe" in Christ?
7. Why can your relationship with Jesus never be broken according to John 10:27–28?

## CHAPTER 3

# THE HOLY SPIRIT OF PERFECTION

### Situation Number One

The baserunner, taking his normal lead from first base, dares a throw from the pitcher. As the pitcher makes his move toward the plate, the baserunner takes off for second base. Each powerful stride brings him closer to another steal. Other teams have had little success in stopping him during the season. His confidence is high. The catcher snaps a perfect throw to the shortstop on the base but the baserunner's "educated" foot safely slips past the tag. The shortstop, determined to jar the runner's confidence, slaps his glove across the runner's face. Stunned, the baserunner jumps to his feet swinging. He's the same player who, an hour earlier, talked to one of his teammates about his new life in Jesus Christ.

### Situation Number Two

The basketball player, at the free throw line, has one shot to tie the score, sending the game into overtime. Ten thousand fans silently cheer him on in this game against their arch rival. Victory will be more meaningful to him than the conference championship. Two days ago he told someone how peaceful the Christian life is. Now his heart is beating like a drum and his legs feel like marshmallow sticks. Where has all his peace gone? Why isn't he calm? Why does he want someone else to take the shot?

What happened to these two athletes? They were supposed to be new men in Christ.

> "Therefore, if any man is in Christ, he is a new creature; the old things [like anger and fear] have passed away; behold, new things have come."
>
> (2 Corinthians 5:17)

The experience of these two players is not uncommon. Most likely you have experienced it You really want to live the Christian life but on the playing field or in the arena it doesn't go smoothly. The moment you believed in Jesus Christ and became a Christian you were given all the power you will ever need to live above anger, worry and fear. We will now see how God enables you to experience the fullness of that power in your athletic performance.

Let's begin by coming to grips with two basic truths concerning your life as a Christian. These truths are better seen as we draw two analogies from a sad experience of Jim Peters, one of England's greatest marathon runners.

The event was the 1954 British Commonwealth Games in Vancouver. Peters had a two mile lead as he entered the stadium to run the last leg of the grueling twenty-six mile race. Then things began to happen. His confident smile faded to a look of desperate bewilderment. Dizziness racked his brain and his body responded with staggering steps. He fell to the ground trying desperately to crawl toward the finish line. Then he couldn't crawl another inch. His "sure" victory ended abruptly two hundred yards from the finish line!

The first analogy regarding the Christian life, in Jim Peters' experience, is that the Christian life is a long distance run.

> "Therefore, since we have so great a cloud of witnesses surrounding us, let us also lay aside every encumbrance, and the sin which so easily entangles us, and let us run with *endurance the race* that is set before us. . . ."
> (Hebrews 12:1)

## Truth No. 1

The Christian life takes endurance. It includes all the second bases you will ever attempt to steal. It includes all the free throws you will ever shoot. It includes all the conversations you will ever have. It includes every moment for the rest of your life.

The second analogy regarding the Christian life, in Jim Peters' race, is that we will fail if we try to live this life on our own power.

A marathon runner must finish the race under his own power. But that isn't true in the Christian life. God did not design the Christian life for you to live in your own power. If Peters could have had a new runner mysteriously enter his body, giving him new strength, he could easily have won the race. Of course, that can't physically happen. But it does happen spiritually in the Christian life.

## Truth No. 2

The Christian life is not a carbon copy of Jesus Christ. It **is** Jesus Christ living His life through us by the power of the Holy Spirit!

The perfect athletic performance is not one in which you try to duplicate the performance of Jesus Christ. It is one in which **you perform like Him because He is performing through you!** It is a supernatural life. The Christian life is doomed to frustration when we try to live it by our own power.

Christianity is not a religion; for, religion is man's attempts to reach and please God on his merit. This is impossible. Christianity is a **relationship with Jesus Christ!** Let's answer five questions to better understand the Holy Spirit's role in making your Christian life and athletic performance work.

## 1. WHERE ACTUALLY IS JESUS CHRIST IN A CHRISTIAN'S LIFE?

Two Bible passages tell where Jesus is at the present time.

> "And after He [Jesus] had said these things, He was lifted up while they were looking on, and a cloud received Him out of their sight. And as they were gazing intently into the sky while He was departing, behold, two men in white clothing stood beside them; and they also said, 'Men of Galilee, why do you stand looking into the sky? This Jesus, who has been taken up from you into heaven, will come in just the same way as you have watched Him go into heaven.' "
>
> (Acts 1:9–11)

The scene was on the Mount of Olives. Jesus had just told His disciples they would be empowered by the Holy Spirit (Acts 1:8) and they would spread His good news throughout the entire land. Then, before their eyes, He disappeared in a cloud. This event, known as the Ascension of Jesus, marked the end of His physical ministry on earth for the time being. God sent two messengers to give added information to the amazed onlookers. They said Jesus **would return to earth** "in just the same way as you have watched him go into heaven." He has not yet returned. If Jesus left earth, but has not yet returned, where is He now? We're given the answer in the second of these two passages.

". . . Christ Jesus is He who died, yes, rather who was raised, who is at the right hand of God, who also intercedes for us."

(Romans 8:34)

Jesus Christ is alive. He is at the right hand of God. To sit at the right hand of anyone was considered the place of honor. Jesus Christ is presently with His Father in the place of highest honor. His purpose is to intercede on our behalf. Just as a lawyer represents you to a judge, Jesus represents you to His Father. He is away from earth in His glorified body awaiting His return.

But He does have **fellowship** with each Christian. He promised before He left earth, "And I will ask the Father, and He will give you another Helper, that He may be with you forever . . ." (John 14:16). This "Helper" is also called the Holy Spirit in John 14:26.

## 2. WHO IS THE HOLY SPIRIT?

The Holy Spirit is the third Person in the Triune God. He is God just as Jesus Christ is God. When Jesus told His disciples the Father would give another "Helper, that He may be with you forever . . ." (John 14:16), He gave us the identity of the Holy Spirit. The word "Helper" describes the role that the Holy Spirit is to have with the Christian. The same Greek word describes Jesus in I John 2:1 when it is translated "Advocate." It's a word describing a person who is called alongside another to help. Jesus said this would be "another" Helper. There are two Greek Words that can be used for the word "another." The first word describes something that does the same thing but is different in nature. For instance, you can use a baseball bat as a hammer to pound a nail. Both the bat and a carpenter's hammer will pound the nail, but they differ in nature. The bat is made of wood while the hammer is made of metal.

The second word describes something that does the same thing and is exactly the same in nature. It is this word that Jesus used for "another" to describe the Holy Spirit. The Holy Spirit is a person the same as Jesus is a person! He is God just as Jesus is God!

## 3. WHAT DOES THE HOLY SPIRIT DO?

The more aware you are of the Holy Spirit's activities, the more you will appreciate His importance. Here are a few of His activities:

**A. He gives us insights as we read the Bible. He also recalls Jesus Christ's teachings to our mind.**

"But the Helper, the Holy Spirit, whom the Father will send in My name, He will teach you all things, and bring to your remembrance all that I said to you."

(John 14:26)

**B. He convicts people of their sin** (missing the mark of God's perfection).

"And He, when He comes, will convict the world concerning sin, and righteousness, and judgment."

(John 16:8)

**C. He guides us in God's Truths.**

"But when He, the Spirit of truth comes, He will guide you into all the truth; for He will not speak on His own initiative, but whatever He hears, He will speak; and He will disclose to you what is to come."

(John 16:13)

D. **He confirms we are God's children.**

"The Spirit Himself bears witness with our spirit that we are children of God."

(Romans 8:16)

E. **His major role, however, is to form Jesus Christ in You!** Paul wrote in his letter to the Galatians,

"My children, with whom I am again in labor, until Christ **is formed in you** . . ."

(Galatians 4:19)

The phrase "Christ is formed in you" is our big clue concerning the Holy Spirit's major role. The word "formed" is *not* the same word that would describe molding a lump of clay into an object. Rather, it is the same word we would use to mean, "The running back is in good form today." We mean the running back showed the ability he was capable of showing. He lived up to his potential. His outward action accurately expressed his inner athletic ability. Paul told his readers that he was waiting for the day when their outward actions fully reflected Jesus Christ. He wrote "formed" in the passive voice which means it is an action done by someone else. Those Galatian Christians were not able to reflect Jesus Christ on their own power or determination. That is the role of the Holy Spirit. Other passages to look up concerning His work include: John 15:26; Acts 1:16; 2 Peter 1:21; Acts 16:6–7 and Romans 8:26.

## 4. WHEN DOES THE HOLY SPIRIT COME?

The Holy Spirit enters your life the very instant you believe in Jesus Christ and accept Him into your life. His main purpose is to reflect Him through your thoughts and actions. To do this He must come to you the **very same moment** you believe in Christ. If you don't have the Holy Spirit you don't have Christ. You are not even a Christian! If you have Christ, you have the Holy Spirit. It is impossible to have one without the other.

> "... But if anyone does not have the Spirit of Christ, he does not belong to Him."
>
> (Romans 8:9)

## 5. HOW WILL THE HOLY SPIRIT MAKE ME DIFFERENT?

One of the most important areas of His work in your life is the area of attitudes. Paul writes about these attitudes.

> "But the fruit of the Spirit is love, joy, peace, patience, kindness, goodness, faithfulness, gentleness, self-control ..."
>
> (Galatians 5:22–23)

Your athletic performance can be one of the most difficult areas to experience Christ's attitudes. Athletic competition draws out natural attitudes faster than most other areas of our lives. On the other hand, the athletic performance can be one of the greatest showcases for your new attitudes.

The "fruit of the Spirit" Paul writes about to the Galatians is nine attitudes of Jesus Christ. What difference would you see if you had the fruit of the Spirit? Let's see how each of the nine attitudes, in the fruit of the Spirit, can affect your athletic performance.

**Love** is the first listed. It's most outstanding quality is self-sacrifice. With love comes the willingness to give completely of yourself for another person. You'll discover in chapter ten how to unleash your love for Jesus Christ through your athletic performance.

You'll experience a new intensity in your actions because of love's self-sacrificing quality.

**Joy** is the attitude of gladness. It does not change when circumstances change. Joy is grounded in confidently knowing God is in full control of all circumstances. When you are emotionally unhappy, you can have the attitude of gladness, or joy, because your reliance is on God. You know His purpose is being carried out. The attitude of joy is especially important for the athlete whose position on the team is not yet determined. It gives you confidence through injuries and other set-backs that God will work it all out for His purpose.

**Peace** does not mean that you will be problem-free. It refers to a calm as you deal with the problems. It comes when the Holy Spirit gives you God's perspective. Let's say that you don't have a statistically good game. As a baseball player, you strike out four times. As a football player, you fumble the football three times. As a golfer, you shoot twenty over par. The world has not ended! The Holy Spirit will give you God's perspective on how that performance ties in with His overall plan. You'll have His peace because you'll have His perspective.

**Patience** refers to your slowness to anger even when given bad treatment. A pitcher deliberately throws the ball at you. Your normal tendency would be to charge him, trying to drive the bat down his throat. Most likely your concentration on the game would be destroyed if you continued in the game. But the Holy Spirit gives you an attitude of calmness. You don't get angry. You're able to concentrate on the job ahead.

**Kindness** actually refers to a calm dealing with other people. Angry voices can surround you but you will remain calm. You can even calmly talk to them. This attitude demonstrated in the heat of competition really shows the power of the Holy Spirit.

**Goodness** is the attitude that demonstrates you are more interested in a person's inner worth than his physical attractiveness. It's a tremendous characteristic to have in better understanding both teammates and opponents. Our tendency is to be overly impressed by one's physical prowess, forgetting that your opponent is human. It's also our tendency to pay attention only to people who measure up to a certain standard. For instance, the seven foot high jumper gains greater approval than the one who jumps six feet. This attitude of goodness sees a person for who he really is. Team unity is developed upon this attitude.

**Faithfulness** is a vital ingredient for any team athlete to have. It is the attitude of reliability, enabling another person to trust you. When you say some thing, it's as good as done.

**Gentleness** is the attitude of looking out for someone else's best interests. You do whatever is beneficial for that person. This attitude will give you a great place of value on your team. You'll have a desire to help others, not to win their favor, but because the Holy Spirit directs you.

**Self-control** is the attitude of mastery over your desires and impulses. It helps develop proper training habits as well as protect you from influences that could distract you from God's best.

The Holy Spirit is sent from God to conform your attitudes to those of Jesus Christ. If you don't have His attitudes, you are **not** controlled by the Holy Spirit at that particular moment. When He is controlling your mind, all the new attitudes listed in Galatians 5:22–23 are in you.

We'll next take a look at your responsibility to the Holy Spirit that enables you to remain under His control.

## FOR DISCUSSION

1. How does the Jim Peters race relate to your Christian life?

2. What influence has the Holy Spirit had upon you today?

3. In what ways have you found it difficult to experience Jesus' attitudes in your athletic performance?

4. To what degree has the "fruit of the Spirit" in Galatians 5:22–23 affected your athletic performance this past week?

## CHAPTER 4

# THE CHRISTIAN ATHLETE'S RESPONSIBILITY TO THE HOLY SPIRIT

If it is the Holy Spirit's work to mold you into the likeness of Jesus Christ, what responsibility do you have in the Christian life? To better understand your responsibility, we'll use the analogy of the athlete and his coach. A good friend of mine, John Warder, developed this graphic analogy for a group of California athletes. I'm sure you will find it to be as helpful as I have in understanding this responsibility.

The coach has a responsibility to draw out the potential within the athlete. The athlete, on the other hand, has a responsibility to **respond** to the coach's guidance and direction. Let's say your coach tells you that if you placed yourself totally under his control you will become an All-American or All-Pro. You would have to make a decision, wouldn't you? You could choose to try to develop your own skills and hope for the best or you could put your trust in your coach's guidance and leadership. Choosing the latter, you would have a responsibility to give him your total allegiance in following his guidance and leadership. It would be his responsibility to give you the right direction. You both have a tremendous responsibility.

The same kind of partnership is ours with the Holy Spirit. The moment you believed in Jesus Christ and accepted Him into your life, the Holy Spirit was sent by God to you personally. His role is to guide and direct you toward maximum development as you're conformed to the likeness of Jesus Christ. The Holy Spirit develops within you a hunger for learning God's Word and a new desire for doing things God's Way. Three of His greatest tools are **God's Word in the Bible, prayer and Christian fellowship.** He inwardly makes His wishes known to you. Sensitivity and obedience to His promptings result in maturity as a Christian. Apathy and direct disobedience to His leading result in a frustrated Christian life resembling the ups and downs of a roller coaster!

The baserunner and free throw shooter in the preceding chapter were not controlled by the Holy Spirit. Their attitudes did not reflect His leading. The Holy Spirit works together with **God's Word in the Bible.** He teaches us things about Jesus through the Bible just as a coach teaches his style of play through words and drawings. When you're sensitive to the Holy Spirit you're sensitive to God's thoughts and actions He has for you.

## CONTROLLED BY THE HOLY SPIRIT

There is a strong bond between a coach and the athlete who responds enthusiastically to his coach. It's easy to "second guess" your coach. But it is the wise athlete who puts himself totally under the control and leadership of a coach in whom he has confidence. The temptations to "second guess" him will occasionally come. It takes a conscious effort to be sensitive to the coach and totally obedient to him. Your willingness to do what your coach asks of you frees him to do his best job. You have a responsibility to submit to your coach's leadership. Ephesians 5:18 explains a similar responsibility regarding your relationship with the Holy Spirit:

"... be FILLED with the Spirit ..."

In the athletic world you do things to get certain results. For instance, you can increase your effectiveness as a pass receiver with hand-eye coordination drills. You can increase your vertical jump in basketball with weight resistant exercises for your legs. The more effort you personally put into it, the better will be the results. But in the Christian life, your effort is to continually **rely on the Holy Spirit** for God's power instead of doing things by your own insights and power.

The word "filled" means **controlled.** Paul wrote that as a Christian you are to be **controlled by the Holy Spirit.** Your responsibility is to allow Him to control you. How do you do this? The Holy Spirit works through your mind. Your mind is a human receiving set for the Holy Spirit's direction just as it is for receiving directions from your coach.

Let's return to Paul's statement in Ephesians 5:18, ". . . be filled [controlled] by the Spirit . . ." As you understand three things about this statement, your responsibility regarding the Holy Spirit will become clear.

1. Paul wrote this as a **command.** It is not something that is natural for you to do. A wrestler is about to attempt a double-leg take-down on his opponent. He must consciously think about that move to make it happen.

It takes a conscious effort on his part. The double-leg take-down won't happen by itself. He remembers his coach's instructions and consciously looks for the right opening. As a matter of choice, he makes the move. His coach's direction would not have affected his performance if he would not have purposely followed through with it. In the same way, the

Holy Spirit does not control your mind unless you are consciously alert to His direction.

2. Paul wrote this command in the passive voice which means it is something **you cannot do for yourself.** In baseball, you don't develop your skills as a hitter to the maximum by throwing the ball up in the air and swinging. It's best to have a pitcher working with you.

Likewise, in the Christian life you can't develop to the maximum if you try to do it yourself. The Holy Spirit works with you and sends His thoughts. Maximum development in the Christian life results by staying constantly alert to those thoughts and acting upon them.

3. ". . . be filled [controlled] by the Spirit . . ." is written in the present tense which means **it should be continuously happening.** This control by the Holy Spirit is a moment to moment way of life. It takes place on the football field in the same way it takes place at home.

It's a constant staying alert to the Holy Spirit's guidance and insights.

How does the Holy Spirit control you? Does He live in your legs and arms? Of course He doesn't. When your coach gives you instructions, he doesn't stoop to talk to your feet, does he? He looks you in the eye and talks. Your senses pick up what he says, transmit it to your brain. In turn, impulses are sent to your legs and arms to carry out the action. The Holy Spirit works in much the same manner. The apostle Paul explains the role of your mind in how the Holy Spirit controls you.

> "And do not be conformed to this world, but be transformed by the **renewing of your mind,**

that you may prove what the will of God is, that which is good and acceptable and perfect."
(Romans 12:2)

The word "mind" refers to all of our senses which are alert to external objects—the primary organ being the brain. The human mind, acting independently, can produce great works. But it can also produce chaos. It was designed by God to work in a dependent way with His Holy Spirit.

God is not limited to working through your mind. He is all-powerful and can bring about His will many ways. But it is your mind that the Holy Spirit engages most of the time.

We concluded last chapter with a description of nine **attitudes** you will experience as the Holy Spirit controls your life. Now let's look at three ACTIONS you will experience as the Holy Spirit controls your mind.

vs. 19 ". . . 1) speaking to one another in psalms and hymns and spiritual songs, singing and making melody with your heart to the Lord;
vs. 20 2) Always giving thanks for all things in the name of our Lord Jesus Christ to God, even the Father;
vs. 20 3) and be subject to one another in the fear of Christ."
(Ephesians 5:19–21)

## Action Number One

You will be "speaking to one another in psalms and hymns and spiritual songs, singing and making melody with your heart to the Lord . . ." (verse 19). No, that doesn't mean you'll suddenly become a great singer. It refers to an **outward action** resulting from your **attitude toward God's Word.** Your conversation with other people will be based upon God's thoughts that the Holy Spirit impresses upon your mind. You'll be uplifting others instead of making critical remarks about them and to them. You'll also have a gladness in your heart seen by others in your manner of speech.

## Action Number Two

You will be "always giving thanks for all things in the name of our Lord Jesus Christ to God, even the Father . . ." (verse 20). You'll be able to thank the Lord in every situation, no matter how difficult. It isn't easy to be thankful for a broken leg or pulled muscle, is it? That's because we don't naturally view such things with God's perspective. The Holy Spirit enables you to do that. The phrase, ". . . in the name of our Lord Jesus Christ" means that you would give the same thanks He would give if He were physically in your situation.

Perhaps you just read the starting lineup and your name isn't on it. Your natural reaction might be disappointment and possibly bitterness toward your coach. But the Holy Spirit calls to your mind God's thoughts, "And we know that God causes all things [including not being in the starting lineup] to work together for good to those who love God, to those who are called according to His purpose" (Romans 8:28). You don't know what will come by not being in the starting lineup, but you keep your mind tuned to God's thoughts in the Bible. You await the Holy Spirit's leading. You can thank the Lord for your situation because the Holy Spirit gives you the capacity to trust Him.

## Action Number Three

Another observable action, as you're controlled by the Holy Spirit, is that you will "be subject to one another in the fear of Christ" (verse 21). The "fear of Christ" is an awesome respect for Him. You'll look out for your teammates' benefit more than your own due to your respect for Christ. You know that pleases Him. It will be easy for your teammates to see this outward evidence of the Holy Spirit's control of your life, especially in your athletic performance.

Your awareness of the Holy Spirit's ministry is on the **conscious** level. In the same way, you limit your coach's influence by sitting in a room with ear plugs, you limit the Holy Spirit's influence by not being alert to God's Word, the **Bible.** It is His role to take God's thoughts in the Bible and form your daily attitudes, thoughts and actions.

The Holy Spirit doesn't recall to your mind that which isn't there! Let's say that you missed a practice session in football and a new play was taught. You're in the game when that play is called. There are no time outs left and there isn't time to ask one of your teammates what to do. What do you do? Panic! Your coach is all over you as you trot to the sideline after the play failed due to your lack of knowledge. You try to explain that you weren't at practice the day the play was taught. Somehow he doesn't seem to appreciate your excuse. He lets you know very quickly that as a member of the team you have a responsibility to learn from the coaching staff or your teammates what takes place at missed practice sessions.

In the Christian life you also have a responsibility to know the thoughts of God. As previously mentioned, you know God's thoughts by reading them in the Bible. With His thoughts in your mind the Holy Spirit relates them to your everyday needs and situations. He will prompt you to study the Bible but it is up to you to actually set aside time to do it. Appendix II gives some help in how to study the Bible for effective results. The Holy Spirit will help you understand what you study. He will also recall the thoughts of God at the moment you need them when you are controlled by Him.

Our natural thoughts are imperfect. They miss the mark of God's perfection and the actions they produce are sinful. Sin breaks fellowship with God. You still have a family relationship with Him but close personal fellowship is broken. The same would be true of fellowship with your coach. If your thoughts and actions are not similar to his, you can't have fellowship. The word "fellowship," as it's used in the Bible, is the result of mutual thoughts, interests and pursuing the same purpose with someone else.

Sin, on the other hand, breaks this close harmony with God. It usually takes place one of two ways.

1. It can be a deliberate thought or action. For instance, if you knew your coach desired you to play your position a certain way and you deliberately played it your own way, fellowship with your coach would be broken. You willfully and knowingly rebelled against him. Many times sin is an active rebellion against the control of the Holy Spirit. You know what God desires but you deliberately choose another way. You miss the mark of His perfection.

2. Sin can also be the result of indifference to the Holy Spirit. Indifference breaks fellowship with God the same way it does with your coach. For instance, if you're daydreaming as your coach is talking to you, or couldn't care less about what you hear him say, fellowship is broken.

You're not actively rebelling against him. You're just indifferent. The result is the same, however, as if you did actively rebel against him. You miss the mark of what he desires for you. You still have a relationship with your coach. You are still on his team, but fellowship with him must be restored If you are to experience the maximum closeness in your relationship. The same is true with your fellowship with God. You are still in God's family when fellowship is broken, but that fellowship must be restored for you to experience a maximum closeness with Him.

## HOW TO MEND BROKEN FELLOWSHIP

God tells us how to get back into fellowship with Him:

> "If we confess our sins, He is faithful and righteous to forgive us our sins and to cleanse us from all unrighteousness."
>
> (1 John 1:9)

In order to mend broken fellowship with your coach you must agree with him that your thoughts and actions were wrong and that his way is correct. The word "confess" means to agree with someone. But that's not all. It carries with it the implication of a committed desire to do what God desires you to do.

In our examples in the last chapter, the baserunner and free throw shooter were out of fellowship with God. But they didn't have to remain in that condition. By responding how God wants them to in I John 1:9, fellowship could have been immediately restored. Let's see how they could have handled it.

The baserunner, in Situation Number One, would not have come up swinging if he was controlled by the Holy Spirit during his attempted steal of second base. One of the attitudes, or results, of the Holy Spirit's control of our mind is **patience.** From the last chapter we learned that patience is slowness to anger even when you're given bad treatment. The shortstop was clearly in the wrong. What he did was inexcusable. But the baserunner's reaction tells us he was not allowing himself to be controlled by the Holy Spirit. His reaction did not reflect patience. He took his eyes off God's purpose in the steal and allowed the circumstance to dictate his attitude. Perhaps he was thinking about his own statistics. Maybe he was thinking about how strategic a successful steal would be for his team. It doesn't make any difference what he was thinking if he wasn't controlled by God's Spirit. He was wrong! If the baserunner doesn't restore fellowship with God, he'll still be unsettled with anger long after the incident is over. His attitude might even be to get revenge in some other way on the field. At best, he will feel embarrased in front of his teammates who look to him to be a Christian example.

According to 1 John 1:9, the baserunner needs to **agree with God he was wrong!** This agreement means that he is **determined** to put anger out of his life forever. That doesn't mean he will never get angry again. And, it certainly doesn't mean he can rid himself of anger on his own power.

He then **claims God's promise in 1 John 1:9 to totally forgive him the wrong that broke the fellowship.** ". . . He is faithful and righteous to forgive us our sins . . ." The additional promise in this passage that He will ". . . cleanse us from all unrighteousness" means He will also remove the feeling of guilt because of the sin.

You claim a promise from God simply by **counting it as true!** Take a look at 1 John 1:9 once again. John tells us that "He is **faithful** . . ." The word "faithful" means that God is both **trustworthy and certain.** When He says it you can believe it!

We're talking about restoring fellowship with God in I John 1:9, not entering a relationship. You have a relationship with Him because of Jesus Christ paying the penalty on the cross. You restore broken fellowship with Him by agreeing with Him and accepting His promise of complete restoration.

The baserunner can also admit to his teammates that he "blew it." This will eliminate any pressure he might feel to try to live the Christian life on his own power. It can't be done and he would be doomed to failure if he tried. The Christian life is designed to be lived by the power of the Holy Spirit. One last step for the baserunner to take is an apology to the shortstop.

As the basketball player stood on the free throw line, he felt as if a 2000-pound rock was weighing him down. He knew one inaccurate move of his arms or fingers would throw the ball off course. His rhythm was gone except for the steady beat of his pounding heart. In this situation he can do something about it before he even shoots. His fears should alert him he was playing for the wrong audience. He knows he will let a lot of people down if he misses. He also knows he will receive widespread recognition if he makes it. His mind is not controlled by the Holy Spirit. Remember, the Holy Spirit is always consistent with God's Word in the Bible. God's Word tells him he is to do everything with God as his only audience—not other people.

> "Whatever you do [including shooting a free throw in a game-deciding moment], do your work heartily, **as for the Lord** [your only audience] rather than for men [people in the stands]."
>
> (Colossians 3:23)

The basketball player knows what he needs to do. He wants his fellowship with God restored. Right on the free throw line he can agree with God he was thinking about his own welfare and commit his mind and body to the control of the Holy Spirit.

## FIRST REACTIONS

Your first reaction in any situation can tip you off as to whether or not you really are controlled by the Holy Spirit. Anger released in a temper outburst is not the work of the Spirit.

Fear because of the crowd or game situation is not of the Spirit. Jealousy, indifference to coaches, breaking training rules and critical remarks of teammates are not of the Holy Spirit either. Stay alert to your first reaction. If it is not what Jesus would do: 1) Agree with God what your attitude should be based on His Word; 2) Claim His promise in I John 1:9 that He has removed the barrier between you and Him; 3) Rely on the Holy Spirit to empower you in gaining His perspective once again through God's thoughts in the Bible. Remember, the command, ". . . be filled [controlled] by the Spirit . . ." is given for you to consciously do. To obey any command from God, or your coach, takes a conscious effort. Therefore, you rely on the Holy Spirit by willfully turning your thoughts to God's Word. That is a major part of your responsibility. Then the Holy Spirit will draw your mind to the portion of God's Word you need in your particular situation.

## WRAP UP

The perfect athletic performance can only be experienced by the Christian athlete controlled by the Holy Spirit. You can never perfectly copy the thoughts and actions of Jesus Christ. The Holy Spirit is sent by God to develop Jesus Christ's attitudes and actions in your athletic performance as well as your entire life.

When your fellowship with God is broken because of your indifference to Him, or active rebellion against

Him, restore that fellowship right away according to 1 John 1:9. Perfect actions are the result of perfect attitudes. Perfect attitudes are the product of the Holy Spirit.

## FOR DISCUSSION

1. What are the responsibilities of the coach and the athlete?

2. What are the responsibilities of the Holy Spirit and you?

3. What three things should we know about Ephesians 5:18 and how does that relate to you in your athletic performance? Be specific.

4. What role does your mind have in relation to the Holy Spirit?

5. Discuss three actions that you'll experience as the Holy Spirit controls your mind (Ephesians 5:19–21).

6. In what two ways does sin usually take place? Give examples from your athletic performance.

7. Explain how 1 John 1:9 is used to bring us back into fellowship with God.

8. What do your first reactions usually reveal?

## TALK OUTLINE

- I. There Are Three Basic Truths Concerning Your Christian Life.
    - A. It is an endurance race (Hebrews 12:1).
    - B. It is lived through the power of the Holy Spirit.
        1. This life lived under our power will fail.
        2. Illustrate (Ex. Jim Peter's race).

C. Christianity is not a religion; it is a relationship with Jesus Christ.

II. The Role of the Holy Spirit.
   A. Who is the Holy Spirit?
      1. He is the third person of the triune God.
      2. He is the Helper or Advocate.
         a. John 14:16.
         b. 1 John 2:1.
   B. What does the Holy Spirit do?
      1. He gives insights as we read the Bible (John 14:26).
      2. He convicts people of sin (John 16:8).
      3. He confirms that we are God's children (Romans 8:16).
      4. His major role is to form Christ in us (Galatians 4:19).
   C. When does the Holy Spirit come?
      1. He enters your life the very moment you believe in Jesus.
      2. If you don't have the Holy Spirit, you are not a Christian (Romans 8:9).

III. The Effect of the Holy Spirit on My Athletic Performance.
   A. His most important work is in the area of attitudes (Galatians 5:22–23).
      1. Love.
      2. Joy.
      3. Peace.
      4. Patience.
      5. Kindness.
      6. Goodness.
      7. Faithfulness.
      8. Gentleness.
      9. Self-control.
   B. The Holy Spirit is sent from God to conform your attitudes, thoughts and actions to those of Jesus Christ.

IV. The Christian Athlete Has a Responsibility to the Holy Spirit.
   A. His role is to guide and direct us into our maximum potential as we are conformed to the likeness of Jesus.
      1. He develops a hunger for God.
      2. He uses tools:
         a. God's Word.
         b. Prayer
         c. Fellowship.
      3. He inwardly makes His wishes known to us.
   B. Our responsibility is to be sensitive and obedient to His promptings.
   C. Apathy or direct disobedience results in a frustrated Christian life.

V. According to Ephesians 5:19, It Takes a *Conscious* Effort to Be Sensitive and Totally Obedient to the Holy Spirit.
   A. The word "filled" means to be controlled.
      1. Your mind is the human receiving set for the Holy Spirit's direction.
   B. A conscious sensitivity to the Holy Spirit is not natural; therefore, God made it a command.
      1. It is a matter of your choice—the Holy Spirit does not control your mind unless you are conscious of His direction.
      2. Illustrate (Ex., of coach's instruction).
   C. This is to be a moment by moment way of life.

VI. You Will Experience Three Actions as the Holy Spirit Controls Your Mind According to Ephesians 5:19–21.
   A. Verse 19 refers to an outward action of your words resulting from your attitude toward God's Word.

B. Verse 20 tells us we will be able to thank the Lord in every situation, no matter how difficult it may look.
C. Verse 21 states we will be looking out for the benefit of our teammates more than our own.

VII. You Can Limit the Influence of the Holy Spirit in Your Life.
   A. We must be alert to the Bible.
      1. It is our responsibility to know the thoughts of God (2 Timothy 3:16–17).
      2. Illustrate (Ex., player missing practices).
   B. Sin hinders the influence of the Holy Spirit and breaks fellowship with God.
      1. Sin is deliberate rebellion against God by either thought or action.
      2. Sin is indifference to the Holy Spirit.
   C. We are to mend broken fellowship according to 1 John 1:9.
      1. "Confess" means to agree with God that we are wrong.
      2. "Confess" also implies a determined commitment to please God.
      3. We can be assured of God's forgiveness because of who He is—He is faithful.
   D. Your first reaction in any situation can tip you off as to whether you are really controlled by the Holy Spirit.

## CHAPTER 5

# THE DILEMMA OF A CHRISTIAN ATHLETE

Right after speaking to a group of athletes about how biblical principles relate to their athletic performance, I received a note from one of the athletes in attendance. He wrote, "The most important thing I have learned is that there is a proper motivation for participation in athletics. Previously, without a proper motivation, my performance was **clearly hindered.** Also, without such a motivation, I had been hesitant to even participate."

This note was written by an athlete who discovered the Bible could be applied to his competitive athletic life. But before he made that discovery, he was not experiencing the fullness of his athletic potential. He even considered quitting!

On another occasion I sat in the office of the athletic director of a Christian college. During our conversation he shared that it was not unusual for outstanding athletes to enroll in the college on athletic scholarships and soon quit athletics. Naturally I was curious why this phenomenon kept occurring. He explained that these athletes were not able to relate the Christian life to their athletic performance. It was a conflict and they decided to give up athletics.

Many Christian athletes experience a dilemma similar to this. On one hand, the Holy Spirit is in control and they are experiencing fulfillment in their non-athletic life. On the other hand, there is little or no awareness of the Holy Spirit's control in their athletic performance. This might be your experience.

Let's look at what might be bringing about this frustrating dilemma. One of the things we must consider is your motivation for athletics before believing in Jesus Christ and accepting Him into your life. One of the most common motivational forces is the quest for recognition.

This might have been your motivational force before becoming a Christian. If it was, you might have been able to endure rigorous training sessions that would cause others to quit. The prize of recognition would be yours. Perhaps you wanted attention from a certain girl. Perhaps you desired a professional career.

If recognition was one of your prime motivational forces, you had a great need for personal love and acceptance. You were willing to put all of yourself into windsprints. You most likely didn't even mind the grass drills or running the steps. You knew the price you had to pay for recognition and you were willing to pay it. But what happened when Jesus Christ entered your life? You didn't need the recognition from others anymore. You were loved and accepted by God Himself.

## God's Love

> ". . . and walk in love, just as Christ also loved you, and gave Himself up for us, an offering and a sacrifice to God as a fragrant aroma."
>
> (Ephesians 5:2)

## God's Acceptance

> "Wherefore, accept one another, just as Christ also accepted us to the glory of God."
>
> (Romans 15:7)

Ironically, your athletic performance began to suffer. It lessened in intensity and effectiveness. The motivational force of recognition didn't work for you anymore.

You were trying to train the same way without an intense motivation force. Another factor that might have contributed to your lessened athletic effectiveness is you did not know how to be motivated by Jesus Christ. As a Christian, this could have even led you to question whether or not athletics should remain an important part of your life.

It's common for athletes experiencing this dilemma to make rationalizations during difficult training sessions or competitions. For instance, windsprints might trigger in your mind the need for using that time for Bible study.

Let's consider four facts that will help you understand how you can resolve this dilemma and experience the most effective athletic performance possible for your God-given abilities.

## Fact Number One

**A new dimension was added to your life when Jesus Christ entered!** Nothing was subtracted. Every athlete has at least two dimensions—the mental and the physical. If you are to reach your highest athletic potential, both of these dimensions must be fully developed. Your actual athletic skills are carried out through your physical dimension. However, that dimension can excel only so far as your mind, or mental dimension, drives it. Athletic mistakes are seldom the result of a malfunction of your physical dimension only. Malfunctions, or errors, are usually the result of a lessened intensity in the mental dimension. You can be a great athlete, compared to others, by the full development of only two dimensions. But you cannot become the athlete God intends you to become without the third dimension. This was added when you believed in Jesus Christ and accepted Him into your life. It is this **spiritual dimension** that puts you into a vital and living relationship with God.

This third dimension controls your mental dimension by producing new attitudes—the attitudes of Jesus Christ (Galatians 5:22–23). When you accepted Christ, nothing was taken from your physical or mental dimensions. You have the same muscle fiber, reflex speed, coordination, etc. You have the same potential brain power. But now, you have the ability to communicate with the God of the universe. You have a source of power never before known in your athletic performance. Keep that in mind. You are now a **complete** athlete with the capability of developing and experiencing your fullest potential.

## Fact Number Two

**Your athletic abilities have been given to you by God!** The Bible tells us that "The Lord has made everything for its own purpose . . ." (Proverbs 16:4). The word "everything" includes your athletic abilities. There is nothing that the word "everything" does not include. God invested certain athletic abilities into you for His purpose.

Some athletes have more ability than you. Some have less. Jim Thorpe is considered to be one of the greatest athletes of all time. God invested many athletic abilities into this one man. For instance, in eight years of major league baseball, he compiled a lifetime batting average of .320. He also was an outstanding professional football player and is regarded as one of the greatest all-around backfield players to have ever played the game. In the 1912 Olympic Games, Jim Thorpe amazed the world with his all-around athletic ability by capturing both the five event Pentathlon and the ten event Decathalon. Jim Thorpe had many athletic abilities. Most likely your abilities are not as diversified as his. Yet God has purposely invested in you the exact quantity and quality of abilities He wants developed for His purpose.

> vs. 13 "You made all the delicate, inner parts of my body, and knit them together in my mother's womb.
> vs. 14 Thank you for making me so wonderfully complex! It is amazing to think about. Your workmanship is marvelous—and how well I know it."
> vs. 15 "You were there when I was being formed in utter seclusion!
> vs. 16 You saw me before I was born and scheduled each day of my life before I began to breathe. Every day was recorded in Your Book!"
> (Psalms 139:13–16, The Living Bible)

## Fact Number Three

**You have a responsibility to invest your athletic abilities for His purpose!** Jesus told an interesting story about the use of talents in Matthew 25:14–30. He was talking about money but the truth applies to any raw talent God gives. It includes your athletic abilities.

He said three people were given varying amounts of talents. To one was given five talents, to another two and to the last person, only one. The first two men invested their talents with wisdom and doubled their investments. The person responsible for the one talent did not make use of it. He hoped that his Master would be pleased he didn't lose the talent, but just the opposite happened.

This was his Master's statement: "The man who uses well what he is given shall be given more, and he shall have abundance. But from the man who is unfaithful, even what little responsibility he has shall be taken away from him" (Matthew 25:29, The Living Bible).

As a Christian athlete, you have been given physical and mental abilities for a purpose. You have more than some athletes and less than others. But you do have at least one talent's worth of athletic abilities. God expects you to invest wisely the talents you do have.

## Fact Number Four

**Your athletic abilities, along with all other abilities, can be weapons for God's use.**

> ". . . and do not go on presenting the members of your body to sin as instruments of unrighteousness; but present yourselves to God as those alive from the dead, and your members as instruments of righteousness to God."
>
> (Romans 6:13)

The word "instruments" in this passage has the connotation of being a weapon. Have you ever thought of yourself as a weapon? The world in which we live is a **battlefield** for the war between God and Satan.

> "Finally, be strong in the Lord, and in the strength of His might. Put on the full armor

> of God, that you may be able to stand firm against the schemes of the devil. For our struggle is not against flesh and blood, but against the rulers, against the powers, against the world forces of this darkness, against the spiritual forces of wickedness in the heavenly places."
>
> (Ephesians 6:10–12)

Satan desires to control your mind as does the Holy Spirit. That's why the apostle Paul wrote:

> "And do not be conformed to this world, but be transformed by the **renewing of your mind,** that you may prove what the will of God is, that which is good and acceptable and perfect."
>
> (Romans 12:2)

Weapons are instruments used to bring about victory for one side against the other. That's how God desires you to view the members of your body which includes your athletic abilities. Since the mental dimension controls the physical dimension, it's extremely important that your mind is controlled by the Holy Spirit. The battlefield where this war is waged between God and Satan is your home, school, athletic arena, etc.

This passage also tells us that unless you are a weapon for God's purpose, Satan can and will use you to bring about his purpose. You are either a weapon to do God's will or Satan's will. The choice is yours!

You shouldn't experience a dilemma in your athletic life, as a Christian, if you understand these four facts. An athlete once told me, after hearing the four facts above, "My athletic life has not been in Christ's control. It's been my thing up until now. I want it to be Christ's from now on. I want to give my abilities, whatever they might be, back to Him."

You might feel the same way. You'll notice throughout this entire book there are only two prayers of commitment. In chapter two you were given the opportunity to express your belief in Jesus Christ and to express your desire for Him to control your life. We'll conclude this chapter with a similar opportunity for you to make a commitment to God through prayer. This time it concerns a dedication of your athletic abilities to be used for God's purpose.

Commitments are never to be taken lightly. If you desire to commit your athletic abilities, regardless of their quantity or quality, to be instruments (weapons) for God's purpose, the rest of this book is for you. As I mentioned in the Introduction, this is a handbook. It is NOT to take the place of the Bible in your Christian life. It is designed only to get you started to understand more clearly how the Bible relates to your athletic performance.

## PRAYER OF COMMITMENT

> "Lord, I realize I have been in control of my athletic ability. Right now, I give to You the complete control of the members of my body, including all of my athletic abilities. They are Yours. I commit them to be weapons for Your use. Amen!"

Your Christian life can be a daily adventure. It is exciting because it is lived by Jesus Christ through you in the power of the Holy Spirit. You will experience more of that new dimension and excitement in your athletic performance as you now learn how to compete God's way.

## FOR DISCUSSION

1. Have you experienced this dilemma? If so, how has it affected your athletic performance?
2. What are the three dimensions of a Christian athlete? Explain what influence each has in relation to the other two.
3. How does the story of the talents in Matthew 25:14–30 relate to your athletic performance?
4. Explain how you are either a weapon for God's use or Satan's use.

**GOD'S WORD IN THE BIBLE IS DESIGNED TO RE-PROGRAM YOUR MIND. WHEN HIS THOUGHTS ARE YOUR THOUGHTS, THEN HIS ACTIONS WILL BE YOUR ACTIONS.**

> "And do not be conformed to this world, but be transformed by the renewing of your mind, that you may prove what the will of God is, that which is good and acceptable and perfect."
>
> (Romans 12:2)

## CHAPTER 6

# THE PERFECT GOAL

Since the beginning of sports, men and women have been driven to excel. What prompted athletes in the early Olympic Games to endure painful and agonizing workouts? Was it only an olive wreath? Hardly! The olive wreath placed on a champion's head was only a symbol of the real prize. Champions, amidst great public acclaim, received a life-time income tax exemption. Their children were given a free education. They received many other honors in their home towns.

And today? What has athletes striving to be the best? Today the olive wreath of professional sports is the six figure yearly salary with fringe benefits. The amateur athlete's olive wreath is worldwide travel and national acclaim.

Athletes are willing to endure great pain if the prize is rewarding enough. To the coach's charge, "Pay the price!" the calculating athlete is thinking, "What do I get?" Every athlete needs a goal of great value to draw him to his maximum performance. But, it must be an attainable goal. Otherwise, he might become frustrated and completely lose heart. Setting the proper goal is one of the most important things an athlete can do.

Finding just the right goal is a delicate matter. Athletes have a tendency to set one that is either too easy to accomplish or one far beyond their ability. Since your athletic goal is so basic in maximizing your athletic performance, let's define what we mean by the word "goal."

## A GOAL IS SOMETHING TOWARD WHICH YOU AIM.

An archer draws his bow string and aims for the bull's-eye of the target. He's not aiming at the tree some 20 yards to the side. His goal is the small black circle in the center of the target. His chance of hitting it depends upon how well he aims.

What you're aiming at, in your athletic career, will determine the caliber of athlete you will become. The proper goal can turn an average athlete into an outstanding athlete. Setting athletic goals is often done with reckless abandonment to the facts relating to an athlete's ability.

For instance, if you set your sights below your potential, you would never maximize your athletic talent.

Perhaps at a baseball game you are impressed by the first baseman. On the basis of that impression you decide you're going to be a major league first baseman just like your hero. You go after baseball with all the enthusiasm of a hungry lion going after a piece of raw meat. Athletic tests reveal you would have been better suited for a career in basketball. You short-circuit a successful athletic career by aiming at the wrong goal.

What's your goal? Perhaps you want to win the conference championship. Maybe you just want to make the team. It's fairly safe to say that, whatever your present goal is, you are not being stretched to the maximum God has in store for you.

Improper goals can leave you empty. An amateur wrestling team had its sights set on a very important contest. Everything the wrestlers did was pointed toward that contest. It came. They did well. Then it happened. Each of these wrestlers experienced a tremendous letdown. They were in an emotional valley. Another important contest was only two weeks away. But, because of this letdown, they were not able to revive to be at their best for the tournament. The goal toward which they aimed lifted them to a peak only to drop them with a thud. Improper goals can do that.

Improper goals can also hinder your performance in other ways. They can tighten your reflexes so that your moves become exaggerated. Aiming toward a long established record falls into this category. One of the most amazing performances of consistency is Joe DiMaggio's great 56 game hitting streak in baseball. Imagine yourself as having hit safely in 20 straight games. Your eyes are on DiMaggio's record. You're taking your final turn at bat in the 21st game. You have walked twice and flied out once. Do you feel any pressure? Maybe you feel only a little. Right? Let's extend your hitting streak to 50 games with the same situation in the 51st game. Now, how's the pressure? The record is so close and yet so very far! Chances are your swing would be a little tighter than if you were just taking your natural cut at the ball.

An improper goal is one that hinders your maximum development. It's common to set our sights on goals to bring us maximum personal satisfaction rather than maximum development. Most goals fall into this "self-satisfying" category. One of the more common is the conference championship. Let's see how this goal, and others like it, can work against your maximum development. Let's say your reason for setting the conference championship as your goal is for the recognition a champion receives. It tingles your ego. That's the problem!

One of the dangers of a self-satisfying goal is when the going gets tough, through pain and exhaustion, your natural tendency is to ease up or quit.

This brings you immediate satisfaction. Although you get personal recognition as a conference champion, you also get personal relief when you ease up or quit. Both bring self-satisfaction. Whichever drive is stronger at the moment will control you. In the heat of practice and competition, relief from pain and exhaustion can momentarily overshadow the satisfaction of a conference championship. Your maximum athletic development is delayed in that moment of easing up.

For example, as a football player, you've just completed the main part of your practice. You're energy is drained. Then you hear a voice bellowing through a megaphone. Your coach yells, "Line up for 20 all-out wind sprints! Remember the championship!" You think to yourself, "Oh no! It's throw up time again!" At this point you aren't thinking about the championship, are you? Maybe after a shower you'll think differently, but that won't help with the wind sprints. You just want to collapse in a swimming pool. That would bring more satisfaction at this point than being named "athlete of the year." If your heart is not in the wind sprints, you won't receive maximum benefit. Your potential for this day has been stifled by a self-satisfying goal.

Only one goal can release a Christian athlete's potential in every practice session and competition. Only one goal can make you desire to run wind sprints with an all-out effort when your body screams for relief. It is not a self-satisfying goal, although there is much pleasure involved. The perfect goal focuses your attention on God rather than yourself.

God's athletic goal for you is to **conform you to the same likeness as Jesus Christ** through your athletic performance. I shared this with a distance runner of national caliber. He thought it was ridiculous. He couldn't see any possible connection between becoming the best distance runner in the land and conforming to the likeness of Jesus Christ. He was right! Chances are there is no connection between being the best distance runner in the land and conforming to the likeness of Jesus Christ. But there is a connection between becoming the best distance runner **he was capable of becoming** and conforming to the likeness of Jesus Christ. We talked for awhile and he was willing to try it. He told me later that, as he practiced focusing his attention on conforming to Jesus, running was becoming more fun. But listen to this!

He cut over 45 seconds from his BEST time in the six mile run within a 30-day span. Did he suddenly get new ability? No. He just released the ability he already had. Needless to say, this Christian runner was convinced that God's goal was far superior to any he had ever set for himself.

You might never win a conference championship as you conform to the likeness of Jesus. Maybe you don't have that ability. God's goal for you does not lift you beyond your ability. Neither do other worldly goals. God's goal enables you to experience the **fulfillment of your ability.** My distance runner friend summed it up when he said, "Great times and honors might come as a result of being conformed to the likeness of Christ but should never be an end in themselves."

## BIBLICAL PREMISE FOR GOD'S PERFECT GOAL FOR YOU

> "For whom He foreknew, He also predestined to **become conformed to the image**

> **of His Son,** that He might be the first-born among many brethren."
>
> (Romans 8:29)

God desires you to become just like Jesus. This is a continuous process of development that will one day reach its fulfillment. There is coming a day when you WILL be just like Jesus. Think about that. You will share in His glory and be in His very presence. It will be a lot different from the pains, exhaustions, misunderstandings and shortcomings you now experience. It will be an historic event.

> "Behold, I tell you a mystery; we shall not all sleep, but we shall be changed [to His likeness], in a moment, in the twinkling of an eye [the fastest possible measure of time], at the last trumpet; for the trumpet will sound [marks the return of Jesus to earth], and the dead will be raised imperishable, and **we shall be changed.**"
>
> (1 Corinthians 15:51–52)

Not only is this historic day coming, but God has given us the **responsibility** to spend more time thinking about it than we would any upcoming competition. He goes so far as to **command** us to make that historic event the dominant theme of our thought life.

> "Therefore, gird your minds for action [having your mind controlled by the Holy Spirit], keep sober in spirit [being sensitive to the Holy Spirit's guidance], **fix your hope [attention] completely on the grace [divine love] to be brought to you at the revelation [actual appearance] of Jesus Christ.**"
>
> (1 Peter 1:13)

It's so unnatural for us to think about this great event, isn't it? We've got too many other things on our mind. Yet, take a look at what's in store for us by making this our disciplined practice.

> "Beloved, now we are children of God. And it has not appeared as yet what we shall be. We know that when He appears we shall be like Him, because we shall see Him just as He is. And everyone who has this hope fixed on Him **purifies himself just as He is pure.**"
>
> (1 John 3:2–3)

The practice of focusing your attention on being in the very presence of Jesus will fill your mind with **new attitudes.** That's the purity about which John wrote. Pure attitudes are the building blocks for pure actions. It was the attitude of Jesus that brought Him through punishing physical torment that would have stopped other men in the starting blocks.

> ". . . for the **joy** set before Him [His attitude of wanting to please His Father above everything else] endured the cross, despising the shame, and has sat down at the right hand of the throne of God."
>
> (Hebrews 12:2)

You must have Jesus' attitude in your athletic performance if you are to conform to His likeness. This is a result of the Holy Spirit controlling your mind. The Holy Spirit will show you from God's Word how Jesus would size up the situation.

You will **never** be able to duplicate the actions of Jesus in your athletic performance on your own power. Only the Holy Spirit can duplicate the performance of Jesus through you. Your responsibility is to become sensitive to the Holy Spirit.

## GOD'S GOAL FOR YOU DEVELOPS YOUR MAXIMUM POTENTIAL

Let's return to those 20 wind sprints on the football field. Everything is physically the same. You're still completely drained of energy. There are two differences. Your goal is to conform to the likeness of Jesus as you run the wind sprints and your mind is picturing that day when you will actually be with Him. You desire to run those wind sprints with all the enthusiasm Jesus would have in your situation. You might end up crawling the last few wind sprints, but even that would be as fast as you could possibly crawl. At that particular moment on the field, your opportunity to conform to the likeness of Jesus is in running the wind sprints. Later it will be something else, such as spending time with your family or studying.

God's goal for you is neither too easy nor is it out of reach. You'll experience it every time you set your mind on the attitude Jesus would have in your situation. The more time you spend reading about Him, the more you will get to know Him. It's the same in developing any friendship. The more time you spend with a person in communication, the better you get to know him. In time, you begin to sense what his thoughts would be in different situations. You have an advantage with Jesus you don't have with other people. The Holy Spirit actually will recall to your mind what His thoughts would be. As you read about Jesus in His biographies (Matthew, Mark, Luke and John) the Holy Spirit will be at work implanting His thoughts into your mind.

### WHAT ABOUT INTERMEDIATE GOALS?

I recall a conversation with a Christian athlete who had made outstanding achievements in his sport. He asked, "I understand that my ultimate goal is to be conformed to the likeness of Jesus Christ, but can't I have an **intermediate goal,** such as the Olympic Games? There's nothing in the Bible that says I can't is there?"

He asked a good question. Let me give a definition of what he meant when he said "intermediate goal" before sharing how I answered him. An intermediate goal is simply something toward which you aim that **will draw you closer toward your ultimate goal.** It's a step along the way. Since this athlete's ultimate goal was to be conformed to the likeness of Jesus Christ, any legitimate intermediate goal would have to draw him closer to that likeness. If it didn't accomplish that, it would not be a valid intermediate goal. Now, let's see how I answered him.

I said, "Olympic Games, league championships, personal honors, specific distances and times, etc., are **not** legitimate intermediate goals. They don't relate to helping you become like Jesus Christ in your athletic performance. You won't find any biblical principle for bringing recognition to yourself as an end in itself. Jesus was a great example of this. His words and actions were designed to draw attention to His Father—not Himself. That's why He summed up His life with the words to His Father in prayer, "I glorified [brought recognition to] Thee on the earth, having accomplished the work which Thou hast given Me to do" (John 17:4).

Let's ask the question a different way. Is there a place for such events as the Olympics, conference play-offs, etc., in your **planning** if your only goal is to be conformed to the likeness of Jesus in your athletics? **Yes, there is!** However, they are not legitimate intermediate goals since they don't directly conform you to the likeness of Jesus Christ. Even so, there is a definite place for them in your planning if you have the caliber of ability to make training for them realistic. We have limitations when we size up our own abilities. We either think we have more than we do or less than we do. It's a good idea to get the analytical opinions of several other people to arrive at a good assessment of your abilities.

There is a big difference between striving toward the Olympics, and other personal honors, and simply experiencing them as a result of your ability. Olympic tryouts, league play-offs and pro tryouts are events that are scheduled on a calendar. God has given us information on how to look upon specific events that are geared to a time schedule.

> "Come now you who say today or tomorrow we shall go to such and such a city and spend a year there and engage in business and make a profit. Yet you do not know what your life will be like tomorrow. You're just a vapor that appears for a little while and then vanishes away. Instead you ought to say, 'If the Lord wills, we shall do this and do that.' "
>
> (James 4:13–15)

An athletic paraphrase of this passage could be:

> "Come now you who say next year I shall make the Olympic team and achieve a specific performance. Yet you do not know God's intent for your athletic talent. You're just a vapor that appears for a little while and then vanishes away. Instead you ought to say, 'If the Lord has designed the Olympics as part of His plan for my life, I shall make the team by peaking for it.' "

Planning is Biblical. It is Biblical that you plan your workouts to arrive at a peak performance for specific events whether they be the Olympic tryouts, league play-offs or some other specific competition. However, it is **unbiblical** to drive toward such events as either your ultimate or intermediate goal. You might be found putting your energies into something that God never wanted for your athletic career. What a tragedy that would be. What a waste of time in the long run.

But let's look at the picture from another slant. Although such events are not to be your goal, it could be that God has designed your athletic career to experience them. There's nothing wrong in planning your training program to peak for a scheduled event. It becomes wrong only when you allow it to take your mind off your ultimate athletic goal of conforming to the likeness of Jesus. Keeping the proper balance is the key. That's difficult to do. Jesus warned us of danger in striving toward God's purpose while pursuing something else from our own desires, such as the Olympics.

> "No man can serve two masters, for either he will hate the one and love the other, or he will hold to one and despise the other. You cannot serve God and mammon."
>
> (Matthew 6:24)

The word "mammon" refers to anything that is not of God. It usually is of a material nature. Jesus referred to a person, trying to do things God's way, while having desires not from God. It's impossible to serve God and yourself at the same time. Jesus could just as well have referred to the athlete wanting to conform to His likeness while, at the same time, peaking for a certain event. Because that event brings pleasure, he finds his thoughts are focusing more on it than on becoming exactly like Jesus in his athletic performance. It started as just another event in his over-all program but ended as his true athletic goal. In other words, it became "mammon."

## HOW TO KEEP YOUR EYES ON GOD'S GOAL FOR YOU

One way to keep God's goal focused sharply is to review the purpose for each practice session and competition. This needs to be done before you get to the dressing room. Your athletic purpose is to conform to the likeness of Jesus, having His attitudes and action. **Your goal is not to improve your performance!** Most likely it will improve. However, the improvement will be the result of maximizing your abilities as you conform to the likeness of Jesus.

Each practice session and competition should be viewed two ways. Both of these will help you become like Jesus in your athletic performance.

1. View your performance as an **opportunity** for God to do whatever He chooses. Let's say that you enter the shot put event of a track and field meet. If you place first, you'll earn a spot on a national team that will travel to Europe. You have never been to Europe and you would really enjoy this trip. You're in second place with one throw remaining. The athlete in first place has already finished. It all comes down to one last effort. You uncork one that has a good chance of putting you on that plane to Europe. You can't believe your eyes when it lands just short of the first place mark.

What's your initial reaction? If you had your sights set on that trip in Europe, you would be disappointed. Yet, if your only goal was to conform to the likeness of Jesus, you would see this as an opportunity for God to work His purpose.

> "And we know that God causes all things [even a second place shot put finish] to work together for good to those who love God,

> to those who are called according to His purpose."
>
> (Romans 8:28)

God is never stymied by circumstances. If He wanted you in Europe, He could have had you put the shot further. **God either causes or allows things to happen for His purpose.** He is never surprised by the results. A professional football player summed it up best when he said, "When I give my all for Him, the results will be His best for me." Although His purpose might not be clear right away, each of your performances are simply opportunities for God to do whatever He chooses.

2. View each practice session and competition as a **two-way evaluator.** First, they evaluate to what degree you really are performing like Jesus with his **attitudes and actions.** Remember, it's impossible to be a carbon copy Jesus. You will only experience this conforming process as you consciously allow the Holy Spirit to do it through you.

Let's say you are a wide receiver in football. You want to perform like Jesus, but every now and then you relish the recognition you'll get for making a spectacular catch. Your play is called in a crucial situation. You can already see the headlines spreading word of your heroics. At the snap of the ball you begin your pattern. You know you can get clear. You're in the open with no defender within ten yards. The ball is fired toward your glue-like fingers. Just as you are about to haul it in you hear the gentle footsteps of a charging "bull elephant." Your opponent and the ball arrive simultaneously. The ball whizzes over your head but the defender doesn't.

He nearly breaks you in two. Curse words fly out of your mouth. Is that how Jesus would have responded? Of course not. This tackle evaluated what your goal really was on the play. You were hunting for the headlines of man rather than desiring to conform to the likeness of Jesus. Your first reaction in any situation is usually a good evaluator if you are living that moment God's way.

Do you let that failure stifle your desire to perform like Jesus the rest of the game? No! Just honestly agree with Him that you were wrong according to 1 John 1:9. Set your mind back on what your real purpose is—to conform to the likeness of Jesus—and MOVE ON!

The second way practice sessions and competitions evaluate you is **physically.** You will not always be at the same physical level of performance due to such factors as rest, nutrition and possible injuries. A careful analysis of your training results can help avoid the pitfall of over-training common to so many athletes.

## A FINAL WORD

Most goals athletes set for themselves are self-satisfying. Such a goal can never stretch you to your maximum potential. When the going gets tough in a training session, the point usually comes when your self-satisfying goal gives way to your most immediate self-satisfying tendency. Most of the time this means you will ease up. Your goal has "sold you out!"

The only goal that can release you to your maximum potential, moment by moment, is the one God has set for you. Your goal is to conform to the likeness of Jesus so that you perform exactly like He would perform in your situation.

You will reflect His attitudes and actions. His perfections become your perfections through the power of the Holy Spirit. The more you think about the day when you will actually be in His presence the more you will experience this conforming process take place in your athletic performance.

## FOR DISCUSSION

1. Define what is meant by the term "goal" relating it to your athletic performance.
2. What have been some of the results from setting improper goals?
3. What is the danger of setting self-satisfying goals for your athletic performance?
4. What is God's *only* goal for you as an athlete? Where is this found in the Bible?
5. Why should our focus be on the return of Christ? What affect can this have on your athletic performance?
6. Discuss what the relationship must be between intermediate goals and your ultimate goal.
7. Discuss how such events as conference championships, Olympics, etc., relate to biblical planning.
8. Discuss what two ways you should view your practice sessions and competitions.
9. How do you handle wins and losses in view of your ultimate goal?
10. Do you believe God *causes* or *allows* you not to win first place? Why?

## CHAPTER 7

# WINNING IN THE PERFECT ATHLETIC PERFORMANCE

A rookie baseball pitcher named Harry Hertman, playing for the Brooklyn Dodgers, is believed to have had the briefest major league career of all time. It all happened in 1918 on that long awaited day when he made his first appearance in a major league game. It was against the Pittsburgh Pirates. What a day. The first batter he faced singled and the next one tripled. Rattled a bit, he walked the next batter. Then the final blow came when the clean-up man singled. Hertman was quickly replaced by a relief pitcher. After showering and getting dressed, the distraught pitcher headed for a recruiting station and enlisted in the Navy, never again to be heard of in baseball. The baseball career of Harry Hertman came to a sudden end!

It would be wrong to conclude that Hertman did not have ability as a pitcher. He would not have been signed to a major league team if the scouts had not thought he could make it. Other pitchers have been hit harder than Hertman. Perhaps he wanted to enlist in the Navy all along. However, let's pose this question. Could his problem have been not so much a lack of ability as it was a lack of the right perspective on winning and losing?

If it was, Harry Hertman is just one of thousands of athletes who was hindered in his athletic performance because of a wrong perspective on winning and losing. Let's see what God's perspective is on this subject. As we do, you'll see how His perspective on winning and losing frees you to consistently perform at your maximum capacity.

## COMMON DEFINITIONS HINDER YOUR PERFORMANCE

The most widely accepted definition of winning is to "defeat your opponent." If we turn 180 degrees the other direction, we find that the common definition of losing is to "be defeated by your opponent."

These definitions have been ingrained in us from childhood. Every time we read a sports page, or hear the results of recently played contests on radio and TV, we come across this definition of winning and losing. Most every newspaper has a "win-loss" column in the sports section. It keeps records of the various sports in season. This statistical way of measuring the effectiveness of an athlete or team helps to ingrain in us this widely accepted definition of winning and losing. Bold print goes to the athlete who defeats the rest of the field. We seldom read much about those who have been defeated.

In the following three hypothetical situations you'll see how these common definitions of winning and losing can hinder your athletic performance.

### Situation Number One

You are a tennis player training for an opponent who has not been having a good season. You've been enjoying a very successful season with many victories and few defeats. There is no doubt in anyone's mind that you are the better athlete. How would you train for the upcoming competition against your weaker opponent?

- ☐ I would train just as determined and disciplined as I would if I were going up against the conference champion.
- ☐ I would be a little less disciplined in preparing for this competition.

You know you can lay off the whole week and still beat your opponent. If your definition of winning is to "defeat your opponent," and that's all you are preparing to do, chances are great you won't be very disciplined in training for this competition. Your athletic ability is fully developed by maximizing your training sessions, not by letting up when the opposition isn't a threat.

## Situation Number Two

Imagine yourself as a wrestler well behind in a match against a stronger opponent. He not only is stronger than you, but he also has superior techniques and speed. You're behind 15 to 1 with two minutes remaining. What would your attitude be in this situation?

- ☐ I would still be going all-out toward defeating him.
- ☐ I would have lost some of my desire to go on.

Proverbs 23:7 gives us some good insight as to what your actions would be if you were mentally letting up: "For as he thinks within himself, so he is." This means what you have on your mind will eventually surface in your actions. If you slacken your mental intensity, your physical actions will show it. You're capable of releasing more of yourself but you don't because you have no hope of defeating your opponent. Athletic ability is improved only when that ability is exercised. Again, the common definition of winning has allowed circumstances to dictate how much of your ability will be exercised.

## Situation Number Three

You are a baseball player coming to bat against a well known pitcher regarded as the best in the league. He knows that he's good and he confidently glares at you as you step toward the plate. You aren't the best hitter in the league. In fact, you aren't even the best on your team. You've had poor results against him in the past and you're presently in a batting slump. What would be your attitude as you face him?

☐ I would be confident that I would get a hit

☐ I would be wondering if I would even see the ball.

Nervousness usually causes a loss of timing, rhythm and coordination. It's the confident athlete who consistently produces the best. The common definition of winning tells you that you must get a hit off him. It causes you to focus your attention on the pitcher rather than the execution of your skills.

The Bible gives us God's perspective on winning and losing. It's different from the world's interpretation of them. As you make His perspective yours, you will be free to always do the best you are capable of doing.

## GOD'S PERSPECTIVE ON WINNING AND LOSING

**Winning is the total release of all that you are toward becoming like Jesus Christ in each situation.**

**Losing is not releasing your entire self toward becoming like Jesus Christ in each situation.**

What a difference this is from the long ingrained definition of winning and losing. When you have

God's perspective on winning and losing, circumstances will not control your athletic performance. Three Bible passages are used as building blocks upon which His perspective is based.

## Building Block One

> "Whatever you do, do your work heartily as for the Lord rather than for men."
>
> (Colossians 3.23)

The word "whatever" includes **everything you do In your particular athletic performance** whether it is running, throwing, jumping, etc. The word "heartily" means you do it by **totally releasing** all of your abilities toward the task at hand. It involves much more than just your strength. For instance, if you were a golfer ready to stroke a two foot putt, you would be leaving your mental abilities behind if you pulled back your putter and drove the ball with all of your strength. "Heartily" refers to your **mental and physical abilities** as well as your **emotional energies.** If you are a baseball player and hit away with the bunt sign on you would not be totally releasing yourself, even if you did get a hit. **Obedience, concentration, reflex action, strength, speed, strategy, enthusiasm** are all wrapped up in the word "heartily."

If we were to stop at this point it would sound pretty much like the philosophy, "Just give it all you've got and you're a winner!" But we're not going to stop here because God doesn't. That is **not** what Colossians 3:23 says. **It is not just a matter of "giving it all you've got!"** It's doing it "as for the Lord rather than for men." **Jesus Christ is your only audience!** We so often perform for other people—girlfriend, fans, coaches, scouts, TV cameras, etc. We want their approval.

When the bleachers are filled with people, or a certain person is there, most athletes can really give of themselves. It all depends on how much the recognition of others means to the competing athlete. But what happens when only a few people come to see the competition? What happens if that certain person isn't there? Some enthusiasm is gone, isn't it? We are oriented toward a human audience to the point it can stifle our athletic performance if the crowd isn't large enough or if that certain person isn't there.

Picture Jesus Christ as the only one in the stands. That's how God wants you to perform. He wants you to picture Jesus Christ as your only audience. What a thrill it would be to perform only for Him. Colossians 3:23 says whatever you're doing in your athletic performance is to be done with the **total release** of all that you are.

## Building Block Two

> "And whatever you do in word or deed, do all in the name of the Lord Jesus, giving thanks through Him to God the Father."
>
> (Colossians 3:17)

Here again, we have the phrase "whatever you do." Again it includes everything you do in your role as an athlete. How are you to do it? Do it all "in the name of the Lord Jesus." This phrase means **you are to totally represent Jesus by saying and doing only those things He would say and do.** It means you are to have His attitude in everything you do in your athletic performance. You can see how important it is to get to know Him as you study the Bible. Without knowing Him, you cannot possibly consistently have His attitudes.

### Building Block Three

> "Therefore we are ambassadors for Christ, as though God were entreating through us . . ."
>
> (2 Corinthians 5:20)

You are an ambassador of Jesus Christ. An ambassador is someone who **represents** another person or organization. Our country has ambassadors to other countries. Their role is to say and do those things that the leadership of our country would say and do in the situation. **You are Jesus Christ's personal representative in everything you do,** whether you are throwing a ball, running, jumping thinking, speaking, etc.

Let's get the full flavor by putting our three building blocks together in an athletic paraphrase.

> "Since you are an ambassador for Jesus Christ (2 Corinthians 5:20), you are to conduct yourself in word and action how Jesus Christ would conduct Himself (Colossians 3:17). Do whatever you do with a total release of your mental and physical abilities and your emotional energies toward performing like Jesus, having in mind that Jesus is your only audience" (Colossians 3:23).

## THE PREMISE FOR GOD'S PERSPECTIVE ON LOSING

God's perspective on losing is based upon an historic event in the early Christian church. It was a time when Christians, in an act of love, were selling their possessions and pooling the money to benefit other Christians in need.

> "But a certain man named Ananias and his wife Sapphira sold a piece of property, and kept back some of the price for himself (with his wife's full knowledge). And bringing a **portion** of it, he layed it at the apostles' feet. But Peter said, 'Ananias, why has Satan filled your heart to lie to the Holy Spirit, and

> to keep back some of the price of the land? While it remained unsold, did it not remain your own? And after it was sold, was it not under your control? Why is it that you have conceived this deed in your heart? You have not lied to men, but to God.'"
>
> (Acts 5:1–4)

We don't know what prompted this couple to sell their property. Whatever it was, they decided to sell all their land, but to give only a portion of it to the church. It was their privilege to hold back some money for their own benefit, but they made a serious mistake in claiming it was the full amount when they gave it. Ananias and his wife tried to **fake it.** This should be a real eye opener since athletes tend to do the same thing. Do you remember the last time you didn't really put everything you had into your athletic performance? Often our natural tendency is to hold back even before we feel fatigue and pain. We can fake it with other people but we can never fake it with God. There is no way you can perform like Jesus without completely giving all you have at a given moment. Jesus gave all He had whether He was teaching, counseling, calming a storm or being crucified because **He wanted only to please His Father and do His will!**

A loser is an athlete who does not give a total release of all he is to perform like Jesus. You can defeat your opponent 50 to 1, setting a new record in the process, and still be a loser from God's perspective. Neither the score nor the circumstances have anything to do with it.

## A TOTAL RELEASE PERFORMANCE BY JESUS CHRIST

God has not only defined winning, but He has demonstrated a **winner** in action. Let's take a glimpse of the action at a place called the Garden of Gethsemane. The setting is shortly before Jesus was taken to the cross to undergo a torturous death by crucifixion.

At approximately 11 o'clock in the evening, Jesus and eleven of His men made their way toward a familiar spot, at the base of the Mount of Olives, known as the Garden of Gethsemane. Jesus left eight of His men by the garden entrance, and took three of them toward the center with Him. After a few minutes He left them, and going a little further, He fell to the ground in complete agony. It was in the cool of the evening, yet sweat was pouring off His body. As He lay on the ground He yelled out, "Father, if You are willing, please take away this cup of horror from Me" (Luke 22:42, The Living Bible).

Jesus used the word "cup" to refer to this particular portion of His life. He was saying He didn't want to go through with the crucifixion if there could be another way to accomplish His Father's purpose.

**There is nothing wrong with desiring to quit.** Every athlete has within him that desire when the going gets extremely difficult. The natural tendency is to quit. How you handle that desire determines if you are a winner from God's viewpoint. Let's see how Jesus handled His agony.

He was heard to say, "But I want Your will, not Mine" (Luke 22:42, The Living Bible). Not only do we have the command (Colossians 3:17, 23) to give a total release toward becoming like Jesus Christ, but we have the perfect example of Jesus giving a total release of Himself in the Garden of Gethsemane. **He totally released Himself to do His Father's will even when it meant He would experience great pain, death and total separation from His Father!**

A very brutal scene was next in store for Jesus only a few hours later—the Roman scourge. It was another situation that would reveal His **winning** character.

Any person scourged by Roman soldiers was handled in one of two ways. In both of these ways the prisoner was stripped to the waist. Either he would be bent over and tied to a stake, or he would be placed on the ground face down, arms and legs spread. Whichever was used, the result was exactly the same. The Roman soldier administering the scourge would have a whip of three or more thongs. The thongs would not be very long in length, but on the end of each would be a sharp implement of stone, metal or jagged bone. Sometimes pieces of lead would be tied on to the thongs, giving them additional weight and destructive force.

The person doing the scourging would hit the victim about the base of his neck and quickly pull the thongs, with the sharp implements imbedded in the flesh, down the length of his back. One medical authority, having done research applying the Roman scourge to cadavers gives us some insight as to the pain. He said that between the eighteenth and twenty-fifth lash the victim would have his skin torn completely off his back. A few more lashes would cut up his flesh so badly you could actually push the flesh apart and see portions of the internal organs.

The Bible reveals to us that Jesus went through this painful experience without a whimper. Once again we see the **winning** character of Jesus as He totally released Himself toward His Father's purpose and relied on Him in this situation. **Although He had the desire to quit, He yielded Himself completely to His Father's purpose for Him, rather than give in to His own desires.** Jesus proved Himself to be a winner through the Garden of Gethsemane ordeal and the painful Roman scourge. Yet, there was still a greater test to reveal His character. It took place on a hill outside the city of Jerusalem.

One historian said that **crucifixion** was the most cruel way of putting a person to death. Basically, there were two ways to crucify someone—each producing the same excruciating pain. In the first way, the person would be staked or tied to the cross laying on the ground. The cross and his body would then be lifted and plunged into the hole, in the second way, the vertical beam would already be planted in the ground. The individual would be staked or tied to the horizontal beam which would then be lifted and dropped into a slot on the vertical beam. The Bible indicates that Jesus was staked to the cross, thereby experiencing more pain than if He were tied.

In both common methods of crucifixion, the victim's shoulders were dislocated when the cross dropped into place. With dislocated shoulders, the victim could not pull the weight of his body up to relieve pressure on his lungs. Breathing was extremely difficult. In fact, the only way that he could adequately breathe was to push his torso upward by straightening his legs. With force against the spike through his feet, he could maintain this "breathing" position for only a few seconds. Then, because of the awkwardness of the position, he would collapse until he began gasping for air again. The victim became a human yo-yo as he kept moving up and down in this fashion. The victim's body would be wracked with convulsions by extreme changes of body temperature caused by a mal-functioning nervous system. The Romans could keep such a person alive for days, making this perhaps the most torturous way of putting anyone to death.

Jesus could have kept Himself from this torturous death. He could have chosen not to have gone His Father's way. By simply denying He was God, His prosecutors would have dropped their case against Him and the crucifixion would not have occurred. At any point Jesus could have quit. Yet, He was totally releasing Himself with all He had toward God's purpose for Him in this particular situation.

At 3 P.M., what He feared most in the Garden of Gethsemane the evening before, took place. He cried out with great pain, "My God, My God, why have You forsaken Me" (Matthew 27:46, The Living Bible)? At this particular moment in history, God the Father totally separated Himself from His Son. Why? It was at this moment in history that Jesus paid the penalty for every wrong you and I have ever committed against God! Jesus totally gave Himself for you and me at this moment. At any point Jesus could have turned back from His mission, but He was a **winner.** Jesus accomplished His purpose for going to the cross.

## GOD USES EACH SITUATION

If you give a total release of yourself toward becoming like Jesus in your athletic performance, you will never look on a defeat from an opponent as a loss. It is a **learning situation** in which more of your potential can be brought to the surface. Remember, from the world's viewpoint, when Jesus hung dead on the cross, it looked as though He had been defeated and was a loser. Yet, this provided a setting for the greatest event in history to take place. On the third day, He defeated death and was raised from the sealed and guarded tomb where they laid Him. His resurrection from the dead demonstrates the power available to us enabling us to live above our circumstances.

## DON'T COMPARE PERFORMANCES

People tend to compare your present performance with those of the past or expectations of the future. Don't let that sway you. What you have will vary from time to time due to sickness, injuries, rest, etc. Your responsibility is to give what you do have, not what you don't have. Your only comparison is with Jesus Christ. Let's say as a quarterback you previously completed 19 out of 21 passes. The next time you complete only 6 out of 30 passes. Did you let down?

Perhaps, but not necessarily. Statistics depend on game conditions, etc. God's perspective on winning depends only upon how you perform in relation to how Jesus would have performed.

You can have a 9.5 clocking in the 100 yard dash to your credit and then run only a 9.9. You can still be a winner from God's viewpoint. On the other hand, you can be a loser even if you statistically bettered your best performance. It depends entirely on how much of yourself you released to perform like Jesus with the same attitude and intensity He would have.

You will never be sidetracked by the score, your opponent or any other factor if your only thought is to represent Jesus as you are empowered by the Holy Spirit. Your only thought will be to please the Father in all that you say and do. As you perform in this manner, you can also know with confidence that the results of the competition will be His to bring Him honor!

### FOR DISCUSSION

1. How has the world's definition of winning and losing hindered your athletic performance?
2. How has God's perspective on winning and losing helped your athletic performance?

3. What effect do attitudes have on your actions according to Proverbs 23:7?
4. Explain in detail how Colossians 3:23 relates to your athletic performance.
5. Explain why Colossians 3:23 is not "just giving it all you've got."
6. How does the phrase "do all in the name of the Lord Jesus" (Colossians 3:17) relate to your athletic performance?
7. How does being an "ambassador for Christ" affect you and your athletic performance?
8. Explain how you can be a loser from God's perspective after defeating your opponent.
9. Discuss the qualities of Jesus Christ as He went through Gethsemane, the scourge and the crucifixion. Then discuss what your athletic performance would be like if you display those qualities.
10. How are you to look upon a defeat by an opponent when you've given a total release?
11. God expects us to give **all** that we have, not what we don't have. What effect has this had on your athletic performance?
12. What can you be assured of when you give a total release?

## TALK OUTLINE

I. Having the Right Perspective on Winning and Losing Will Free Us to Be Consistent to Perform at our Maximum Capacity.
   A. The world's definition of winning is to defeat your opponent.

B. The world's definition of losing is to be defeated by your opponent.
   1. Illustrate how these definitions can hinder your athletic performance (use three examples mentioned).
   2. According to Proverbs 23:7, your mental intensity will be revealed through your physical actions.

II. The Bible Gives God's Perspective on Winning and Losing.
   A. Winning is the total release of all that you are toward becoming like Jesus Christ in each situation.
      1. Building Block No. 1 (Colossians 3:23).
         a. Describe the word "whatever."
         b. Describe the word "heartily."
         c. This is not a philosophy of "just giving it all you've got."
         d. Jesus Christ is your only audience.
      2. Building Block No. 2 (Colossians 3:17).
      3. Building Block No. 3 (2 Corinthians 5:20).
      4. You are Jesus Christ's personal representative in everything you do.
   B. Losing is not releasing your entire self toward becoming like Jesus Christ in each situation.
      1. The biblical premise for losing is Acts 5:1–4.
         a. Our natural tendency is to hold back even before we feel pain and fatigue.
         b. You can never fake out God.
         c. A loser is an athlete who does not give all he is to perform like Jesus.
         d. Illustrate (ex. beating your opponent—athlete of the year, etc.).

III. Total Release Performance by Jesus Christ.
   A. His winning action demonstrated in the Garden of Gethsemane.

B. His winning action demonstrated during the scourge.
C. His winning action demonstrated on the cross.

IV. Applications from the Winning Efforts of Jesus.
A. You will never look on a defeat from an opponent as a loss.
B. You are not to compare your present performance with anything or anyone but Jesus Christ.

## CHAPTER 8

# JESUS IN PREPARATION

How would Jesus have prepared for athletic competition? Perhaps this question is not as far removed as one might at first suspect. Athletics are a microcosm of life itself. Athletics contain all the situations that can cause excitement, worry, frustration, fear, elation, depression, etc. If it is true we can learn much about how we handle life by how we handle athletic competition, then the opposite would equally hold true. We should be able to study the characteristics of a person in various life situations to determine how that person would respond in athletic competition. So, by looking at how Jesus lived His life, we can determine fairly accurately how He would have prepared for athletic competition. Although sports were different in His day than in ours, His method of preparation would apply today.

Let's now consider how Jesus would have prepared for athletic competition. Would He have used a different approach for a basketball game than He would have for a football game? Would He have prepared differently for a golf match than He would have for a wrestling match? Would He have sat quietly on a bench in the locker room, contemplating the upcoming action, or would He have stomped up and down on the floor, trying to get "psyched up" for the competition? Would He have cancelled all appointments on the day of competition or would He have been equally available to other people before a game as He would be afterward?

The perfect athletic performance is a result of performing like Jesus Christ. You can never do this on your own power. Only through the Holy Spirit empowering you can have His attitudes, thoughts and actions in your athletic performance.

A study of the life of Jesus Christ draws to our attention at least three different ways He would have prepared Himself for athletic competition.

**1. Jesus would have been in complete harmony with the Holy Spirit!**

One of the greatest dilemmas for a Christian athlete is he experiences the control of the Holy Spirit less on the athletic field than in other areas of his life. He has been used to calling the "shots" in his athletic performance. He continues in a similar manner as a Christian. As a result, he pursues the wrong goal, uses the wrong motivation and is generally insensitive to the Holy Spirit in his athletics.

Satan's main target is your mind. His main objective is to control it. One of Satan's most clever tricks is to keep your mind from being controlled by the Holy Spirit. The Holy Spirit is the source of power for your athletic performance. Jesus was totally sensitive to the Spirit's direction. To understand His dependence on the Holy Spirit, let's look carefully at two examples of how Jesus operated while on earth.

A. Jesus did not rely on His equality with God the Father and the Holy Spirit.

> "Have this attitude in yourselves which was also in Christ Jesus, who, although He existed in the form of God, did not regard equality with God a thing to be grasped, but **emptied himself** [laid aside the use of

> His privileges as God], taking the form of a bondservant [one who is in total subjection to the one above him in a line of authority], and being made in the likeness of men [had to rely on the same source of power as we do]."
>
> (Philippians 2:5–7)

Although Jesus completely demonstrated the personality of God (John 1:18), He did not count on His nature as God to handle daily encounters and difficult moments.

B. Jesus relied totally on the Holy Spirit. Jesus went to a wilderness area immediately after He was baptized. During forty days in this area He prepared for His mission on earth. The point we want to observe is what led Him to that wilderness area. Did He just decide to get away from everyone for awhile? No, of course not. He was led by the Holy Spirit.

> "Then Jesus was **led up by the spirit** into the wilderness to be tempted by the devil."
>
> (Matthew 4:1)

The words "led up" tell us it was not Jesus' independent decision to go to the wilderness area. He was led by the same source available to you in your daily life and athletic performance--the Holy Spirit. You have many mental and physical qualities upon which you could rely, if you should choose to do so. Jesus had many mental and physical qualities also, but He chose to rely totally on doing everything His Father's way. For Jesus, His Father's way was living His earthly life by the power of the Holy Spirit. This is God's desire for you, too.

It's interesting that Jesus, even though totally relying on the Holy Spirit, still did battle with Satan. Your mind has been conditioned by a world controlled by Satan. It still desires trophies and tangible goals such as poundages, distances, etc. You always have a choice, whether to have the Holy Spirit control your mind or simply yield to your natural tendencies.

**2. Jesus would have engaged in effective prayer.**

Jesus prayed to prepare Himself for **every** situation. His practice of prayer was not changed when circumstances changed. For instance, if He were an athlete, we could say that He would have prayed before a practice session the same as before the world championships. It was an exciting time for Him because He knew how to pray. (You'll find many helpful insights for effective prayer in Appendix III.)

Three episodes involving Jesus point out the priority prayer would have had if Jesus had prepared for athletic competition.

**Episode one** involves His routine life. Jesus was very popular throughout the land. If He sought His own recognition, He could have easily maintained a long ego trip. He could not walk down the street without being recognized.

> "But the news about Him was spreading even farther, and great multitudes were gathering to hear Him and to be healed of their sicknesses . . ."
>
> (Luke 5:15)

This sort of day was as routine for Jesus as training sessions are for you. It was the same day after day.

How did He handle it? It would have been easy to be sidetracked from His purpose. His greatest desire was to accomplish His Father's purpose (John 17:4).

The next verse describes what He routinely did to avoid being sidetracked.

> "But He Himself would often slip away to the wilderness and pray."
>
> (Luke 5:16)

Jesus **often** slipped away. It was not just something He did if He faced extreme pressure. It was His regular practice. Jesus also went to the wilderness to pray. The "wilderness" refers to any place where He could be alone. You can have effective prayer in the middle of a football game. But, for the most effective prayer, it's good to get off where there are no distractions.

**Episode two** in Jesus' prayer life takes us to the evening before He chose His apostles from among the large number of people following Him. This was a momentous decision. These were key men He would train to take His message throughout the world. It had to be the right decision. Luke describes how Jesus prepared for making it.

> "And it was at this time that He went off to the mountains to pray, and **He spent the whole night in prayer to God.** And when the day came, He called His disciples to Him; and chose twelve of them, whom He also named as apostles . . ."
>
> (Luke 6:12–13)

Can you imagine praying for an entire night? That's the time for sleep. Yet, Jesus was about to make one of the most important decisions of His life. As He went to His Father for direction, the Holy Spirit led Him to pray all night. Remember, according to Philippians 2:5–7 Jesus completely **emptied Himself** of the use of His privileges as God for His earthly mission. He was in direct communication with His Father through prayer. Through prayer we also have the opportunity to be in direct communication with God.

Jesus was in prolonged prayer before every great decision or event. There will be times when you need to spend much time in prayer. It might be you are thinking about trying out for a team but wonder if you have the time. Or you might need insight in working out a problem with a teammate. These situations don't happen everyday. They didn't for Jesus either. But when such important moments came, Jesus prepared for them in prolonged prayer.

**Episode three** in His prayer life moves us into the Garden of Gethsemane as He prepared for the crucifixion. Jesus approached this crisis event in prayer.

He entered the Garden of Gethsemane with His disciples.

> "And when He arrived at the place, He said to them, 'Pray that you may not enter into temptation.' And He withdrew from them about a stone's throw, and He knelt down and began to pray, saying 'Father, if Thou are willing, remove this cup from Me; yet not My will, but Thine be done.' Now, an angel from heaven appeared to Him, strengthening Him. And being in agony, He was praying very fervently; and His sweat became like drops of blood, falling down upon the ground."
>
> (Luke 22:40–44)

Jesus was honest with His Father when He prayed. Fellowship is at its best when there is honest communication. Jesus actually asked His Father to spare Him the unbearable pain of being separated from

Him. But He also admitted that He above all DID want to do it His Father's way. He was in complete fellowship with His Father all the time. In the same way, you can level with God about your attitude toward practice sessions, the fears you might have, etc. Then, like Jesus, wholeheartedly express your desire to do it His way. Prayer is an excellent opportunity for you to bring your honest thoughts and attitudes before God. Let Him change those that need changing. The book of Philippians is a digest of attitudes that a Spirit-controlled Christian will have. Paul just finished writing about his attitude toward being conformed to Jesus Christ (Philippians 3:1–14). He then wrote,

> "Let us therefore, as many as are perfect [mature in Christ], have this attitude; and if in anything you have a different attitude, God will reveal that also to you . . ."
>
> (Philippians 3:15)

The Holy Spirit will point out those attitudes to you not pleasing to God. For instance, let's say your opponent is undefeated. He has a great desire to remain that way. You know your only athletic goal should be to conform to the likeness of Jesus Christ through the competition. But you just can't get your mind off your opponent's ability. He is awesome. It boils down to your being afraid of him.

In prayer, because you consciously want the Holy Spirit to control your thoughts, admit your fear to God. Agree with Him that this fear is not of Him. Trust Him to change your attitude of fear. One of the passages the Holy Spirit might recall to your mind is a statement of Jesus in Luke 12:4, "And I say to you, My friends, do not be afraid of those who kill the body, and after that have no more than they can do."

Your opponent will not literally kill you. But the point is clear. Jesus is talking about an extreme. Fear of people comes from our own mind. It is not a result of the Spirit-controlled mind. God is not afraid of people and an athlete controlled by the Holy Spirit is not afraid of people. This does not mean you will necessarily beat your opponent. It simply means, as a result of your responding to the Holy Spirit's dealing with your wrong attitude, you will be free to compete without being mentally shackled by fear.

It's easy in competitive athletics to allow your goal to change from conforming to the likeness of Jesus back to gaining 100 yards in a football game, lifting 400 pounds overhead, scoring 25 points in a basketball game, etc. In prayer, you can express your honest thoughts to God about your statistical goal such as 100 yards, 400 pounds or 25 points. Then, the Holy Spirit is free to disclose God's thoughts from the Bible to you. Again, you can see how important it is to study God's Word in the Bible. It enables the Holy Spirit to recall God's thoughts to your mind.

Honesty involves disclosing what you're really thinking. For instance, are you afraid of the poundage you are going to attempt to lift? You might try to convince yourself you're not afraid, but what is your real attitude? Are you hoping for personal recognition from your performance? Here are a few questions that can get you started in being honest with God in prayer:

1. What value do you place on your personal recognition in the upcoming competition?

2. What is your greatest desire at this moment?

3. What do you fear the most regarding this competition?

4. What do you look forward to the most in the competition?

As you honestly disclose your thoughts through prayer and rely on God to deal with them, the Holy Spirit will reshape your thoughts with those of His. Most of the time He will reshape your thoughts by recalling to your mind portions of His Word you have either read or memorized.

**3. Jesus knew His total purpose.**

Jesus prepared Himself by being continuously alert to His purpose which was to accomplish His Father's will. That alertness kept Him from being sidetracked. For instance, He got up early one morning and left the house while His men continued sleeping. He went in the darkness to a lonely place where He prayed. Soon people from the town were knocking on the door where His disciples were sleeping. They wanted Jesus to heal more people as He had done the evening before. Peter and the rest of the disciples went hunting for Jesus to bring Him back to heal the sick. You would think Jesus would have hurried back as fast as He could, wouldn't you? What a shock it must have been to His disciples when He said, "Let us go somewhere else to the towns nearby, in order that I may preach there also; for that is what I came out for" (Mark 1:38).

Healing the sick was good. But Jesus' purpose on earth was not to set up a medical practice. His main purpose was to accomplish His Father's will.

Jesus sized up each situation as to how it would be related to accomplishing His Father's purpose. As the time approached for His crucifixion, He was alert as to how the crucifixion would tie into His Father's purpose for Him. Instead of shying away from this difficult event, He pressed forward to meet it. He said, "Now My soul has become troubled; and what shall I say, 'Father, save Me from this hour?' But for this purpose I came to this hour" (John 12:27).

Your one athletic goal is to be conformed to Jesus Christ in your athletic performance. You are His representative (2 Corinthians 5:20).

This conformity includes your attitudes, thoughts and actions. Every competition is an opportunity for more of that conformity to take place.

As an athlete, Jesus would not have focused His attention on circumstances brought about by the competition. He would not have tried to impress someone in the stands. He would not have felt the pressure of beating the cross-town rival. He would not have had his mind dwelt on the fact the game means the championship. He was too aware of His overall purpose to be sidetracked. His overall purpose for any athletic competition would be to accomplish His Father's purpose. God's purpose for you as an athlete is to have all your attitudes, thoughts and actions conformed to Jesus through the power of the Holy Spirit. As Jesus prepared Himself by a continuous awareness of His purpose, so you can prepare for your athletic performance by thinking about God's purpose for you.

## FOR DISCUSSION

1. Discuss how athletics are a microcosm of life.
2. What can you learn from the prayer life of Jesus to help you in your athletic performance?
3. What are some wrong attitudes you've had in athletics (e.g., fear of opponent, recognition for self, wrong goal) and how do you deal with them in prayer?
4. How does continuously being alert to God's purpose affect your athletics?

# CHAPTER 9

# JESUS IN ACTION

It has been said that "nice guys finish last." If that's true, Jesus Christ would never even have made an athletic team. Yet, a study of His life reveals characteristics essential in championship athletics. In fact, His life reveals far more outstanding athletic characteristics than most champions possess. Jesus never jumped center or ran the fast break in basketball He never plunged over from the two yard line or made a devastating block in football. He never experienced the thrill of a home run in baseball or lifted four hundred pounds over His head. But, as we saw in the last chapter, the characteristics Jesus displayed in His lifetime would have developed His physical and mental abilities to the maximum if He were to use them in athletic competition.

The kind of an athlete Jesus would have been would be determined by His physical talent. This we don't know. Those who say that He had the greatest strength, coordination and speed are on shaky ground since the Bible doesn't deal with that issue of His life. Some people say that because He is God He would have the greatest of all power and skill as an athlete. Yet in Philippians 2:6–7 we're told that Jesus emptied Himself of the use of His divine powers and privileges. Paul wrote, ". . . who, although He existed in the form of God, did not regard equality with God a thing to be grasped, but emptied Himself, taking the form of a bondservant and being made in the likeness of men."

He lived His life as a human being, subject to the same physical flaws all humans have. We can be sure of one thing. Whatever athletic ability He did possess would have been maximized. We can say this confidently because of attitudes that shaped His life. Attitudes result in action. His attitudes resulted from a life in total surrender to the Holy Spirit. Mark wrote, "And immediately the Spirit impelled Him to go out into the wilderness" (Mark 1:12). Luke stated, ". . . after He had by the Holy Spirit given orders to the apostles whom He had chosen" (Acts 1:2).

As a result of His control by the Spirit, He engaged in a quality of action that would have made coaches want His services for their teams.

The perfect athletic performance is a result of the Holy Spirit developing you into the likeness of Jesus through your athletics. He will give you the same attitudes Jesus would have had in your particular athletic situation. Those attitudes will produce the same quality of actions Jesus would have had whether He had carried out a blocking assignment, ran the ball, stole second base, attempted a ten foot putt, etc. As we look at Jesus in action, we'll see four attitudes Jesus would have had as an athlete. These will be your attitudes as you allow the Holy Spirit to put them into your mind. The highest quality of athletic performance will be yours as a result. Let's look at each of these four attitudes individually.

**1. Jesus had the attitude of intensity.**

He totally concentrated His thoughts and actions toward His goal of accomplishing His Father's purpose in every situation. ". . . I do not seek My own will, but the will of Him who sent Me" (John 5:30).

> "I glorified Thee on the earth, having accomplished the work which Thou hast given Me to do" (John 17:4).

Jesus was in complete oneness with His Father in every thought and action. He never lost sight of His purpose, no matter how tough the situation became. For instance, one day at noon Jesus and His men came to a water welt in Samaria (John 4:1–42). Jesus was tired and hungry. He had been walking all day and needed a break along with the rest of His men. His disciples went into the nearby town to bring back some food for all of them to eat. Jesus waited for them at the well as He took a breather.

A woman from the nearby town came to draw water from the well. Jesus was tired but instead of keeping to Himself, He initiated a conversation that brought about some indepth interaction. This isn't the natural sort of activity for a tired mind and body, is it? Jesus' attitude of intensity to achieve His Father's purpose in every situation made it possible for this woman and many citizens of the town to come into fellowship with God. When His men came back, they were amazed that Jesus didn't immediately eat the food they brought Him.

> "But He said to them, 'I have food to eat that you do not know about.' The disciples therefore were saying to one another, 'No one brought Him anything to eat, did he?' Jesus said to them, 'My food is to do the will of Him who sent Me, and to accomplish His work.' "
> (John 4:32–34)

It wasn't that Jesus was no longer hungry. But His intensity—His total concentration toward accomplishing His Father's purpose—filled His mind with the priority of the moment. He was so intent that He wasn't aware of His physical need for food. Physical fatigue first begins in the mind. We believe we are tired long before our body actually needs rest. Rest is important. Yet, because our attitude is frequently focused on our own pleasure rather than on completely representing Jesus, we often think we need rest when we really don't. If Jesus would have performed in athletic competition, that same attitude of intensity would have developed His physical endurance to the maximum. There would have been times when He would have definitely had to stop and get physical rest. But that would have been beyond the point of another person's natural tendency to do so.

His attitude of intensity toward His purpose gave Him the determination to handle pain. That doesn't mean it didn't hurt when the skin was ripped off His back in the scourge. He felt the pain of the scourge just as He felt the spikes driven through His wrists. But He endured pain because of the intense attitude He had toward achieving His Father's purpose.

Pain and fatigue were real in Jesus' life. They are real for you in many athletic performances. You will experience times, even though your attention is on Jesus, when fatigue will actually slow you down.

There will be times when pain refuses to let you continue. Jesus also experienced those times. For instance, He fell under the load of carrying His cross.

But, Jesus always gave what He had to give, and not what He could have given if He had no pain or fatigue. You can never give what you don't have. But, you can give what you do have. Jesus refused to let His desire for personal comfort stifle His purpose in a situation. If your attitude is one of intense desire to represent Jesus, you will often find you have more to give than you think.

How would Jesus use this attitude of intensity in a sport such as golf where pain and exhaustion are at a minimum? His attitude of intensity was one of total concentration toward His Father's purpose. Every sport requires concentration. Golf professionals tell us the mental aspect is the major factor in golf. You only see what happens physically when a golfer swings his club. But the swing in golf is like the tip of a giant iceberg in the ocean. You only see a small part of what actually is involved. The vast majority remains unseen. Jesus would concentrate in golf to achieve His Father's purpose for the particular shot. His practice swing would be just as important as the match's final putt.

Where does the point come when it is no longer wise to keep going? When does the attitude of intensity begin to work against you? For instance, if you just sprained your ankle, should you continue to play basketball? If you received a gash over your eye, should you stay in the football game?

The attitude of intensity—total concentration toward your goal—is **never foolish to pursue as Jesus demonstrated it.** Remember, His intensity was toward achieving His Father's purpose in every situation. The attitude of intensity must always have direction toward a purpose. It's impossible to be intense if you aren't moving in some direction. For example, Jesus, needed to endure pain and fatigue in order to achieve His Father's purpose for him in going to the cross.

As a Christian athlete, you share Jesus' purpose for every athletic situation you face. It is to accomplish God the Father's purpose through your attitudes, thoughts and actions as the Holy Spirit conforms you to Jesus Christ. Since the design of any athletic competition is to defeat an opponent, you will strategize and execute to carry this out. Where you differ from an athlete not doing it God's way is in your goal. You will strategize and execute in such a manner that you reflect the attitudes, thoughts and actions of Jesus Christ.

So, how far does Jesus' attitude of intensity go? Let's say that you suffer a broken bone. The doctor says you will risk permanent damage if you should play without a three weeks rest. Most likely you would not be demonstrating Jesus' attitude of intensity by insisting on playing. You probably would not be accomplishing God's purpose in that course of action. You would only be satisfying your own desire to play. In fact, you might even be a detriment to the team because of your inability to produce at your best.

Jesus' attitude of intensity did not pursue any course of action that could not be used to accomplish His Father's purpose. For instance, as He discussed things in the temple with a large group of people, they became extremely angry because He claimed to be God. They decided to treat Him the same way they would treat anyone who blasphemed God by claiming equality with Him. They picked up rocks to throw at Him. Jesus' attitude of intensity was just as great when He hid Himself from them as it was when He later went toward Jerusalem knowing that He would be crucified—a death far worse than stoning. What was the difference? To stone Jesus to death would not have accomplished His Father's purpose because His Father had purposed the crucifixion to take place. He would not have fulfilled several prophecies that told His manner of death.

How would this attitude of intensity show itself in a contact sport such as football? Jesus would never have stood around in practice sessions without a purpose in what He was doing. He would have been constantly learning. If He would not actually have been carrying out an assignment. He would have been listening to His coach or learning from other players. He would have been constantly observing. His mind would not have been focused on the usual pain and exhaustion that's part of football. Instead, He would have carried out each assignment with all the strength, energy, timing, etc., He had. He wouldn't have been worried about comparing Himself with other players or even His own past performance. He would have concentrated on giving everything He did have—not thinking about what He didn't have. This attitude of intensity is yours as you allow your mind to be controlled and empowered by the Holy Spirit who gives you Jesus' attitudes.

## 2. Jesus had the attitude of "flexible rigidity."

Jesus was rigid in totally concentrating His efforts to accomplish His Father's purpose. That never changed no matter how difficult the situation. However, He was flexible as to what action He would take. Jesus hid Himself when He faced opposition, on one occasion, and walked right into the middle of His crucifixion on another occasion. He handled the same type of hostile circumstances with different actions.

When Jesus began His march to Jerusalem, where the crucifixion would take place, His purpose was still to accomplish the will of His Father. His Father's will in this instance was for Jesus to pay the sin penalty on the cross. Jesus remained rigid in this purpose. However, He was willing to change His actions in order to accomplish it. We see this in an episode described by Luke.

> "And it came about, when the days were approaching for His ascension, that He resolutely set His face to go to Jerusalem; and He sent messengers on ahead of Him. And they went, and entered a village of the Samaritans, to make arrangements for Him.

> And they did not receive Him, because He was journeying with His face toward Jerusalem. And when His disciples James and John saw this, they said, 'Lord, do you want us to command fire to come down from heaven and consume them?' But He turned and rebuked them. And they went on to another village."
>
> (Luke 9:51–56)

Jesus had to arrive safely in Jerusalem. It was not His Father's purpose to burn the Samaritans with fire. Instead of insisting on staying where He had originally planned, Jesus went on to another village. It required more stamina for already tired bodies. But his intense attitude toward accomplishing His purpose enabled Him to push onward. He was intent on His purpose and flexible on the means to achieve it.

That same attitude of "flexible rigidity" would have been demonstrated by Jesus in athletic competition. Circumstances would not have dictated the changing of His purpose. He would simply have moved on to accomplish His purpose along another route.

This attitude enables you to reach your maximum development as an athlete in every situation. Let's say that you arrive at the locker room mentally and physically ready to give your best in the game. Then you notice on the bulletin board your name is not listed as one of the starters. If you were not controlled by the Holy Spirit, you would have an attitude of great disappointment. You came to play, not watch. However, if you were controlled by the Holy Spirit, you would realize you could accomplish God's purpose whether or not you were in the starting lineup. God's purpose is never stifled from being accomplished. He could have had you in the starting lineup if that was His desire. Your only responsibility is to totally release all your mental and physical abilities, along with your emotional energies, toward becoming like Jesus in whatever your coach has called upon you to do. You can do that on the playing field or on the bench.

Jesus' attitude of flexible rigidity gives you new actions to take. Along with warming up properly, so you're ready whenever the coach sends you in, you also have the task of keeping yourself mentally ready throughout the game. Your alertness to the game can open your mind for observations to help your team that you might not have had if you were actually in the game.

Let's say that during a practice session your group is just standing around, not taking part in the action. The attitude of flexible rigidity gives you a different course of action. It's like being on the bench during the game. You have a responsibility to learn all you can as you watch. When you are called upon, you will be able to transfer that mental knowledge into physical action. Let's say you are watching batting practice. If you are to be like Jesus in doing this, how would He watch batting practice? Instead of just biding His time before His swings, Jesus would be observing the batter in the cage, trying to learn something that would apply to His own swing. Waiting would not keep Him from improvement. He would use that waiting period to develop His ability.

The same attitude of flexible rigidity applies to converting to a new position, meeting a different opponent than was scheduled or even getting injured. There is no set of circumstances that would stop Jesus from accomplishing His Father's purpose.

**3. Jesus had the attitude of divine perspective.**

This attitude kept Him from dwelling on the odds against Him. Odds are always a human calculation. There is no such thing as odds in the divine perspective. Let's look at Jesus in action as He approached the death of one of His best friends.

Jesus was sent word Lazarus was very sick. In fact, Lazarus' two sisters wanted Jesus to come immediately, trusting He would be able to heal their brother. But Jesus didn't go. That isn't the right way for a good friend to respond, is it? It is the right way if that good friend is seeing the situation with an attitude of divine perspective. His primary purpose was to accomplish His Father's purpose. To do this, Lazarus would have to die.

Two days later Jesus told His disciples they were all going up to Bethany where Lazarus and his sisters lived. His disciples were frightened because Bethany was close to Jerusalem. It was in Jerusalem religious leaders were plotting to kill Jesus. His disciples wanted no part of the action if they could stay away. But Jesus saw this situation from a divine perspective.

They went to Bethany and Jesus talked with the two grieving sisters. Lazarus had died. In fact, he had been in the tomb four days already by the time Jesus arrived. There was no chance of Lazarus coming back to life again. The odds were definitely against it. But, let's remember, odds are human calculations. They have nothing to do with divine perspective. Let's capture this setting.

> "Jesus therefore again being deeply moved within came to the tomb. Now, it was a cave, and a stone was lying against it. Jesus said, 'Remove the stone.' Martha, the sister of the deceased, said to Him, 'Lord, by this time there will be a stench; for he has been dead four days.' Jesus said to her, 'Did I not say to you, if you believe, you will see the glory of God?' "
>
> (John 11:38–40)

Here we see what was in Jesus' mind throughout the entire ordeal. He was intensely moving toward accomplishing His Father's purpose through these circumstances. Now, let's see how Jesus defied the odds.

> "And so they removed the stone. And Jesus raised His eyes, and said, 'Father, I thank Thee that Thou heardest Me. And I know that Thou hearest Me always; but because of the people standing around I said it, that they might believe that Thou didst send Me.' And when He had said these things, He cried out with a loud voice, 'Lazarus, come forth. He who had died came forth, bound hand and foot with wrappings; and his face was wrapped around with a cloth. Jesus said to them, 'Unbind him and let him go.' "
>
> (John 11:41–44)

A man dead four days is not supposed to come back to life again. The odds are just too great against something like that happening. It's physically "impossible." But one having the attitude of divine perspective does not see the odds or impossibility of it. He looks at every situation as an opportunity to totally rely upon God in accomplishing His purpose.

That same attitude of divine perspective would have been with Jesus in athletic competition. He would not have been down if He was behind in the score. He would not have given up hope if He faced an undefeated opponent heavily favored to defeat Him.

It is through seemingly apparent defeat that God's greatest glory shines. Lazarus' death paved the way for his restored life. The crucifixion of Jesus preceeded the great victory of His resurrection. Circumstances would not alter Jesus' confidence. They provided opportunities for His purpose to be achieved. Remember, "If God is for us, who is against us" (Romans 8:31)?

Odds can never be against you, whether you are trying out for a position or going against the national champion.

Your purpose in each athletic situation is to accomplish God's purpose. His purpose is accomplished as you allow the Holy Spirit to conform you to the likeness of Jesus Christ.

**4. Jesus had the attitude of controlled emotion.**

Would Jesus lose His temper in athletic competition? Some people believe He would based on how He chased the "rip-off artists" out of the temple. As we carefully look at that episode, we'll see two things: 1) He did not lose His temper and 2) He used a controlled emotion to strengthen His actions.

Jesus actually chased people out of the temple twice. He began His ministry that way (John 2:14–22) and ended it that way (Mark 11:11–18). He released emotion both times. Both times it was a controlled emotion that gave emphasis to His actions.

Jesus had been in the temple many times prior to either of these episodes occurring. He knew what was going on there. In fact, in the second episode, Jesus came into the temple, looked around and then went back to Bethany where He was staying. He had a whole night to think over what He would do. He didn't return to the scene completely unemotional. He was intent on achieving His Father's purpose by ridding the temple of profiteers.

There was flavor in His actions. He didn't simply walk up to the sellers and say, "Pardon me, but I do believe you're trying to make a profit in My Father's house. That's not right. Now please pick up your things and move on to the marketplace." Do you think they would have done it? No! Jesus knew just what actions were needed to clean up His Father's house. He boldly walked up to the tables and turned them over. He used a scourge the first time to chase out the animals. The second time He drove the buyers and sellers out with His hands. The first time He scattered the sheep and oxen. The second time He would not even permit people to carry containers through the temple. He was a man of action. But He was in full control of what He was doing. By the time He was through, He taught and healed those who were making proper use of the temple as a place to worship God.

In competitive sports Jesus would have used this same attitude of controlled emotion. It would have been controlled because He was never out for His own benefit. He only desired to accomplish His Father's purpose. How can the attitude of controlled emotion be used in your athletic performance? Let's say, as a hockey player, you've just been purposely tripped.

What's your first natural reaction? You want to retaliate and get even, don't you? You want revenge.

The results of such retaliation are disastrous. It could quite possibly give you momentary satisfaction, but let's see what else could happen: 1) You could go to the penalty box and would then be of no value to your team during that time period; 2) You could inflict serious injury on the other player and possibly yourself; and 3) You definitely would fall short of your goal of conforming to the likeness of Jesus Christ.

Here's how you could handle the same situation with Jesus' attitude of controlled emotion. The player purposely tripped you. Your first natural reaction might still be one of retaliation. But, because you consciously desire to have the attitude of Jesus, the Holy Spirit can recall to your mind, "Never take your own revenge, beloved, but leave room for the wrath of God, for it is written, 'Vengeance is Mine, I will repay, says the Lord' " (Romans 12:19). Retaliation is God's business, not yours. Your only goal is to conform to the likeness of Jesus in each situation. You agree with God that your initial idea of revenge is wrong. Although the initial emotion is still in your system, you continue to skate, representing Jesus. That emotion can give your actions more precision.

Instead of emotion working against you, it has been channeled to add greater emphasis to your actions as you subject your mind to the Holy Spirit's control.

The attitudes and actions of Jesus Christ are yours when you are controlled by the Holy Spirit. The quality of His attitudes and actions will develop your athletic ability to the maximum potential for which God has designed it. That development is a result of the Holy Spirit conforming you to the likeness of Jesus Christ in your athletic performance.

## FOR DISCUSSION

1. What is the attitude of **intensity** and how does it relate to your athletic performance?
2. Discuss at what point it is no longer wise to keep going? In other words, when is it right to stop or remove yourself from the game?
3. How does the attitude of intensity relate to one on the bench or standing around during practice sessions?
4. What is the attitude of **flexible rigidity** and how does it relate to your athletic performance?

5. What is the attitude of **divine perspective** and how does it relate to your athletic performance?
6. What is the attitude of **controlled emotion** and how does it relate to your athletic performance?
7. Is it ever right to lose your temper?

**CHRISTIAN ATHLETE'S COMMITMENT**

IN EVERY ATHLETIC SITUATION WHETHER PRACTICE OR ACTUAL COMPETITION, I WILL DEDICATE MYSELF TO GIVE A TOTAL RELEASE OF ALL THAT I AM – MENTALLY, EMOTIONALLY AND PHYSICALLY – TO BECOME JUST LIKE JESUS. I WILL DETERMINE TO CONDUCT MYSELF IN A WAY THAT WILL PLEASE THE LORD RATHER THAN GAIN ANY RECOGNITION FROM MEN.

# CHAPTER 10

# THE PERFECT MOTIVATION

Fans who came to see the 1950 Wanamaker Mile sprang to their feet with thunderous applause. The two runners they came to see strained with every fiber in their bodies lunging for the finish line. This photo finish marked the beginning of an eleven month wait before the winner was confirmed. It was the beginning of a great rivalry between two of the most evenly matched milers of all time. Don Gehrmann, a student from the University of Wisconsin, and Fred Wilt, an FBI man, competed against each other several more times in the following two years. When their rivalry finally came to an end in 1952, Gehrmann had chalked up sixteen victories to five for Wilt. The lopsided number of victories for Gehrmann in no way revealed the closeness of their races. Several races ended in controversial photo finishes as never more than a few yards separated them at the wire. Both of these runners possessed great physical ability. In most competitions between athletes of near equal ability, the winner is the athlete who is better motivated.

Motivation took a man with no hope of ever walking again, because of a terrible automobile accident in 1949, to a victory in the 1950 U. S. Open in golf. Ben Hogan astonished the athletic world with his amazing four stroke victory. Then, in 1953, he became the first player ever to win the U.S. Open, Masters and British Open in the same year.

The Gehrmann-Wilt races and the great Hogan victories were spotlight attractions. People came from all over to see them perform. However, the majority of athletes in competitive sports do not experience such a spotlight. Take, for instance, the basketball player whose name will never become a household word. He enters the dressing room the same time as his teammates. His ankles are carefully taped as though he were star of the team. He attends the pre-game briefing session with everyone else. He goes through the basic warm-up drills with the rest of the team. When the signal is given for the game action to start, he slowly walks to his "home away from home"—the bench. When called upon, he must respond with the same enthusiasm as a starter. But how is it possible for him to enter a game and be as highly motivated to do his best as if he were a starter?

## MOTIVATION IS IN YOUR MIND

Motivation is a mental set. What an athlete is thinking will show in his actions.

> "For as he thinks within himself, so he is."
> (Proverbs 23:7)

This passage points out that true attitudes of a person will surface in his actions. In athletic competition the intensity of his actions will reveal the intensity of his attitudes. Therefore, what an athlete thinks is crucial to his performance. Now we'll look closely at the perfect motivational force. Whether you are a starter in the spotlight, or a bench warmer waiting for action, this motivational force will drive you to your highest level of athletic performance.

## NATURAL MOTIVATIONAL FORCES IN ACTION

Most athletes are driven by the quest for personal recognition. Although there are exceptions, the athlete's desire to find recognition drives him to endure grueling workouts. Recognition comes in many ways. Some athletes get their recognition from being part of a team while others must aim at a personal or world record.

Coaches aware of this motivation force of recognition use it in various ways to generate top performances. The coach might use a variety of other natural motivational forces to fan the flames of recognition. Circumstances usually dictate which of these natural motivational forces to use. Some of the more common are revenge, fear and anger.

All the coach can do is hope he can use the circumstances leading up to a contest in the most productive way.

In 1916, the Georgia Tech football coach couldn't have asked for better circumstances to charge his players to a fever pitch against Cumberland College. A baseball game, earlier in the year, provided the setting. Cumberland College, before a huge crowd, defeated the proud Georgia Tech team. It was a humiliating experience for the Georgia Tech team and their student body. Seeds were planted for revenge. The fall of the year brought football season and a new beginning for Georgia Tech fans. The two schools were to meet again—this time on the gridiron. On that long awaited day, Cumberland wished they had never kicked off. Probably, they also wished they had not defeated Georgia Tech in baseball. Play was finally halted at the end of the third quarter with the score in favor of Georgia Tech, 222–0. Revenge can be a strong natural motivational force if the circumstances are right They were right for Georgia Tech!

Circumstances were also just right for one of the great upsets in Rose Bowl history. Mighty Stanford, undefeated in season play, came into the annual event a heavy favorite over Columbia. This time the setting was provided by California newspapermen who gave Columbia as much chance to defeat Stanford as Custer had going against Sitting Bull. Lew Little, the ever alert Columbia coach, knew how to fan the flames of recognition to get his men primed to play their best ball of the year. In the pre-game team meeting, he simply handed his players various clippings from the California newspapers. The players began to see "red" as they read line after line of copy that ridiculed their ability on the gridiron. If the game wasn't about to start, they might have vented their anger another way. As it was, the underdog Columbia team unleashed its pent-up anger against a surprised Stanford squad. The final score was 7–0 with Columbia's coach proving an angry football team is a potent football team.

## DANGER OF NATURAL MOTIVATIONAL FORCES

Natural motivational forces, such as revenge and anger, have been used to fan the flames of personal recognition. They have accounted for great victories through the years. However, they have also been responsible for great agony and crushing defeats. Although much can be written about the positive results of natural motivational forces, much can also be written about problems they have caused.

For instance, anger triggered a temper outburst that cost a tennis player the match. The angry player disputed a line call to no avail. Instead of controlling angry emotions, the player smashed a tennis ball over the grandstand in an outburst. The match was lost 6–8, 6–8 although victory was within reach in the first set, at set point, only to have a wild volley follow the anger outburst.

Perhaps one of the most dramatic examples of how natural motivational forces can work against us is the women's 400 meter relay in the 1936 Olympic Games. This was the Olympics in which Jesse Owens and friends emphatically did much to upset Hitler and his racial theories. It was also the Olympic Games during which the motivational force of fear stifled a seemingly brilliant performance. The German girls were clearly the favorite. Their closest rival was the American team featuring Helen Stephens, the fastest woman in the world.

In the semi-final heat the favored German team established a new world record. The Americans also won their heat running only seven-tenths of a second slower than the Germans. Going into the finals, the German girls had their strategy well planned to counter the blazing speed of Miss Stephens. Their idea was to have the three fastest girls run in the first three positions hoping to build up such a great lead that not even world record holder Helen Stephens could catch them. It was a solid strategy. That part of it did not backfire. They built a tremendous lead as the spectators roared their approval. But, what was about to happen brought a stunned silence throughout the great stadium.

Marie Dollinger, the third German runner, opened the lead to eight meters while a nervous Ilse Dorffeldt awaited the final baton pass. Bud Greenspan, an award winning film maker who has studied great moments in sports history through the use of film clips, has given insight into the thoughts of the young German girl selected to hold off the charge of Miss Stephens.

Greenspan reasoned that Ilse Dorffeldt became the victim of fear. Two factors seemed to cause it. First of all, he said, she was an eyewitness to the world record Helen Stephens set in running away with the 100 meter championship. Secondly, she began to think that the eight meter lead was not going to be enough to hold off the fastest woman alive. Added to these thoughts was the fact that Adolph Hitler was in the stands with his eyes glued to the young girl about to receive the baton. He looked for this relay team to help revive his dream of German superiority.

With her eyes focused downtrack, Ilse Dorffeldt knew she would have to get away quickly if she was going to hold off Helen Stephens. Disaster was about to strike. She reached back to take the baton from her teammate only to grab air. It was a fear drenched Ilse Dorffeldt that finally grabbed the baton, only to feel it slip through her hands as she began her sprint. The hopes and dreams of a German victory over the Americans fell with that baton. No one will ever know if Helen Stephens could have carried the American team to victory had not this happened. The natural motivational force of fear can cause greater reflex action than one usually has. And, as Ilse Dorffeldt discovered, it can cause athletic tightness to the point of making mistakes. Natural motivational forces such as anger, fear, revenge, hatred and pride can fan the flames of recognition to a certain degree. But they are limited by circumstances. An athlete will not always be angry.

Neither will a team always be trying to redeem an embarrassing moment. The dilemma of motivational forces was best summed up by a professional football player when he said, "I'll admit, you just can't get emotionally up for a game fourteen times a year."

## THE MOTIVATIONAL FORCE OF LOVE

Natural motivational forces are inconsistent because they must rely on circumstances to be effective. A far more consistent motivational force is described in the Bible. It is the basic motivational force of love upon which God operates.

> "For God so **loved** the world, that He gave His only begotten Son, that whoever believes in Him should not perish, but have eternal life."
>
> (John 3:16)

Love is the only motivational force that Jesus taught His followers to use.

> "A new commandment I give to you, that you love one another, even as I have loved you, that you also love one another. By this all men will know that you are My disciples, if you have love for one another."
>
> (John 13:34–35)

One of the reasons love is such a great motivational force is that it draws out the best in a person. When you love someone you want to please that person. For instance, I love my wife very much. That love has given me a desire to please her. I know she likes it when I open doors for her or take the garbage out. Because I know these things please her, I enjoy doing them for her. Love for my wife helps draw out the best in me. It also helps get the garbage out!

Let's say you are a baseball player who has developed a strong, respectful love for your coach. You respect him as a leader and admire him as a man. During practice and games you have a desire to please him, don't you?

If he asked you to run a message for him, you'd jump at the chance. You could have a sore ankle, but you'd walk ten miles in the rain if that's what he wanted. You know that he desires his players to hustle on the field. "Hustle" is your middle name because you want to please him. The quality of your actions for a person reveals the quality of your love for him.

Another reason love is such a great motivational force is that it does not depend upon circumstances. Actions motivated by love are directed toward the one loved. They are not stifled by circumstances surrounding your competition. We have a good example of action motivated by love in the Old Testament. Three of King David's top warriors risked their lives to get him a drink of water from his home town well. David expressed a desire for it out of sentiment, not out of thirst. Here's what happened.

> "Then three of the thirty chief men went down and came to David in the harvest time to the cave of Adullam, while the troop of the Phillistines was camping in the valley of Rephaim. And David was then in the stronghold, while the garrison of the Philistines were then in Bethlehem. And David had a craving and said, 'Oh that someone would give me water to drink from the well of Bethlehem which is by the gate!' So the three mighty men broke through the camp of the Philistines, and drew water from the well of Bethlehem which was by the gate, and took it and brought it to David."
>
> (2 Samuel 23:13–16)

Three men risked their lives to get David a drink of water. You'd think he was dying of thirst. David was a veteran of roaming the hills, leading an army of men. Such a great leader would not bring his men to a campsite without plenty of drinking water available. David and his men had water.

When David's three friends first arrived for their visit, they spent some time talking with each other. Apparently, in the course of this conversation, David reminisced about the cool and good tasting water from his hometown well in Bethlehem. He expressed a craving for it out of sentiment and taste, but never commanded his friends to get any for him.

David's friends left the cave, broke through enemy lines, as they maneuvered their way to the well, and drew a pitcher of water. Their lives were endangered with every step they took. They were probably a battle-worn threesome when they arrived back at David's cave.

All this for a pitcher of water? It doesn't make sense, does it? Do you know what David did when they handed the pitcher to him?

> "Nevertheless, he would not drink it, but poured it out to the Lord; and he said, 'Be it far from me, O Lord, that I should do this. Shall I drink the blood of the men who went in jeopardy of their lives?' Therefore he would not drink it."
>
> (2 Samuel 23:16–17)

David knew his friends didn't risk their lives for a pitcher of water. He knew it was their way of saying, "David, we love you." Most likely he had been their leader since they joined the army. Perhaps that's all he was at first. But after going through many battles together, David became their friend. He cared for them and laughed with them. Most likely he counseled them in difficult times and constantly encouraged these three men. Their respect for David as a leader developed into a love for him as a man. It developed to the point where these three great friends were willing to risk death as an expression of love for him. Intense love toward someone reproduces itself in intense action for that person.

This draws us to one of the chief differences between the motivational force of love and other more natural motivational forces. **Love directs your attention away from yourself!** Natural motivational forces, such as anger, revenge, pride, etc., are designed to bring you personal satisfaction. They can only drive you to the extent that the pain and fatigue you must endure is worth the personal satisfaction you will receive.

## LOVE IN ACTION

Let's take a look at how you, as a Christian athlete, can be motivated by your love for God in your athletic performance. There are four major points to consider as we do this.

1. **You can express your love for God through your athletic performance.** The apostle Paul wrote that, as a Christian, you can use your physical abilities, which include your athletic performance, to unleash your love for God. He wrote, "I urge you, therefore, brethren, by the mercies of God (because of how God demonstrated His love for you on the cross), to present your bodies (consciously commit your physical abilities to God), a living and holy sacrifice (dead to your own interests and alive to God's interests) acceptable to God, which is your spiritual service of worship (the most logical way for you to express your love and reverence to God)" (Romans 12:1).

In this passage, Paul directs the thoughts of his readers to use all their physical talents for God's purpose. Although he did not write with the athlete in mind, your athletic abilities are included in the word "bodies." It's a Greek word that refers to all one's physical characteristics. God desires each Christian to express his love for Him with every ounce of ability he has.

The apostle Paul tells his readers to express the quality of their love for God through their daily actions. He also tells about the motivational force of love in his own life. He wrote, "For the love of Christ controls us . . ." (2 Corinthians 5:14). He meant that just as a water nozzle thrusts water forward with an intensified force, so were all his actions harnessed together and unleashed into a whole new thrust as a response to Jesus' love for him.

In the same manner, you can respond to God's love for you through your athletic performance. The apostle John wrote, "We love, because He first loved us (1 John 4:19). Our love is in response to His love for us. According to Romans 12:1 you can respond to God's love for you by unleashing your love for Him through your athletic abilities. Each practice session and contest can be a worship experience in loving Him.

**2. The quality of your performance will depend upon your awareness to the quality of your love for God.** Jesus was able to endure great suffering because He was fully aware of how much He loved His Father. In the Garden of Gethsemane, drenched with the sweat of agony, Jesus prayed, "My Father, if it is possible, let this cup [portion of My life] pass from Me; yet not as I will, but as Thou wilt" (Matthew 26:39). Notice that Jesus did not want to go through with the terrible suffering He was about to face. However, His awareness of love for His Father enabled

Him to commit Himself to accept the great pain and even total separation from His Father. **The quality of Jesus' actions revealed the quality of his love.** The quality of your athletic actions can reveal the quality of your love for God.

**3. Your love for God is a natural result of your deepening fellowship with Him.** You don't have to sit in a corner, shut your eyes, clench your fists and repeat several times, "I love God! I love God!" David's three men did not stand around trying to conjure up a love for him. Their love grew out of who David was rather than anything the men did. Love for God develops the same way as love for anyone.

The more time you spend with Him the greater you love Him. Appendix I, "The Quiet Time," will offer you insights in how to spend time with God each day.

4. **Based upon 1 Corinthians 13:4–7 you will experience a new quality of athletic performance as you unleash your love for God.**

You will sense a new enduring power ("Love is patient"). You won't purposely call attention to yourself ("love does not brag"). You will look out for the benefit of your teammates and opponents ("It does not seek its own"). Any wrong done to you by teammates, coaches or opponents will not affect your performance because you won't keep a mental record of wrong actions of others ("does not take into account a wrong suffered"). Your attention will be focused on God's perspective in every situation ("hopes all things"). Finally, you will trust God for whatever results come, knowing He always is in control ("endures all things").

Let's close with a brief look at the enthusiasm God desires you to have as your love for Him is expressed through your athletic performance. Jesus once said,

> "And you shall love the Lord your God with all your **heart,** and with all your **soul,** and with all your **mind,** and with all your **strength.**"
> (Mark 12:30)

The word "heart" refers to your complete personality. Your athletic performance will represent the real you. The phoniness of trying to copy someone else is stripped away. You're not trying to live up to someone else's expectations or even your own dreams of greatness. The word "soul" refers to all the vital and living forces that well up within you. All your energy is to be channeled into expressing your love for God through your performance. The word "mind," in this context, does not refer to your brain. Rather, it refers to a thought process. It can refer to the process of consciously thinking about expressing your love for God through the various components of your performance such as running, jumping, etc. You've got to think about it. It wont' come naturally. The word "strength" refers to your actual physical strength. It's a combination of all your physical skills as they combine together to unleash your love for God through your athletic performance.

The quality of your athletic performance is dependent upon the quality of your love for God. Your athletic performance will be maximized as you consciously commit your actions to the purpose of expressing the quality of your love for God.

## FOR DISCUSSION

1. What is meant by the statement "Motivation is a mental set" and how does this affect your athletic performance?

2. What are some natural motivational forces and how have they affected your athletic performance?

3. Why is love such a strong motivational force?
4. Discuss how the quality of your athletic performance reveals the quality of your love for God.
5. How can you express your love for God through your athletic performance according to Romans 12:1 and 2 Corinthians 5:14?
6. How is your love for God developed? How do you see this affecting your athletic performance?
7. Discuss the enthusiasm you will have as you express your love for God according to Mark 12:30.
8. Specifically, how can you begin to show your love for God?

## TALK OUTLINE

- I. Motivation is Essential to Your Athletic Performance.
  - A. Motivation is a mental set (Proverbs 23:7).
  - B. Your true attitudes will surface in your actions (athletic competition).
- II. Natural Motivational Forces.
  - A. They have accounted for great victories (illustrate).
  - B. They have also been responsible for crushing defeats (illustrate).
  - C. Natural motivational forces are inconsistent because they must rely on circumstances to be effective (illustrate).
- III. The Perfect Motivational Force is Necessary for the Perfect Athletic Performance.
  - A. Love is the only consistent motivational force upon which God operates.
    1. John 3:16.
    2. John 13:34–35.

- B. Three reasons love is such a great motivational force.
  1. It draws out the best in a person (illustrate).
  2. It does not depend upon circumstances.
     - a. Actions motivated by love are directed toward the one loved.
     - b. Illustrate (ex., David's man, 2 Samuel 23:13–16).
  3. Love directs your attention away from yourself.
     - a. In contrast, natural motivational forces bring you personal satisfaction.
     - b. They can only drive you to the extent that pain and fatigue you must endure are worth the personal satisfaction you will receive.

IV. You Can be Motivated by Your Love for God in Your Athletic Performance.

- A. You can express your love for God through your athletic performance.
  1. You can use your athletic abilities to unleash your love for God (Romans 12:1, athletic paraphrase).
  2. 2 Corinthians 5:14.
  3. Our love is a response to His love (1 John 4:19).
- B. The quality of your athletic actions can reveal the quality of your love for God.
- C. Your love for God is a natural result of your deepening fellowship with Him.
- D. You will experience a new quality of athletic perfection as you unleash your love for God (1 Corinthians 13:4–7).
- E. God desires enthusiasm in your athletic performance as you express your love for Him (Mark 12:30).
  1. Heart refers to complete personality.

2. Soul refers to all vital and living forces within you.
3. Mind refers to conscious thinking about expressing your love for God in your athletic performance. This won't come naturally.
4. Strength refers to your actual physical strength and abilities.

F. Your athletic performance will be maximized as you consciously commit your actions to the purpose of expressing the quality of your love for God.

# CHAPTER 11

# OVERCOMING NEGATIVE FORCES

A negative force in athletics is anything that has the potential of stifling your athletic performance. Negative forces can surface many ways in your athletic performance—fear, injury, fatigue, pain, anger, preoccupied mind, etc. Your athletic effectiveness is determined largely by how successful you are in overcoming their impact. We'll now see how to overcome negative forces through the motivation force of love. First, let's see how various types of negative forces enter into an athletic performance.

## Example One

Brad, an offensive lineman in football, is racked by the negative force of jealousy. One of the running backs has been glorying in his long runs and he never gives credit to his line for opening the holes. Brad realizes if he and the rest of the lineman did not execute their assignment on each play the running back would not gain more than two yards a carry. Because of the running back's attitude Brad hopes that he will be hit hard each time he carries the ball. This attitude has begun to surface in Brad's own play. He doesn't have his usual aggressiveness. His actions are less intense whenever the running back carries the ball.

## Example Two

The success of Gary's basketball team revolves around his ability to rebound on both boards. He realizes this and most of the time he is able to do a good job. It's only against teams featuring players with "sharp" elbows that Gary thinks twice about aggressive rebounding. Already he has had ten stitches around his eyes. He doesn't want any more. The negative force of fear is his constant companion against such aggressive teams.

## Example Three

Ted is tied for the lead in one of the most prestigious golf tournaments on the tour. As he is about to tee his ball for the final hole of the tournament, he hears a thunderous roar of approval from the spectators around the 18th green. He can only assume his opponent just made a great putt for a birdy. He realizes that in order to tie, he must do the same on a hole that has given him difficulty in the past. The negative force of mental comparison—his opponent's score and his own poor past performance on this hole-begin to weigh heavily on Ted.

## Example Four

Sam knows it's going to take an all-out effort to defeat his opponent and win the national wrestling championship. He's trained hard for the match and he knows his opponent has also. The match begins at a furious pace. Both wrestlers try to quickly take an advantage. They seem to be equal in technique, speed and strength. The only difference is seen as the two athletes rest on their backs a few seconds, awaiting the third period. Sam notices that his opponent does not appear to be breathing nearly as hard as he. Sam is extremely tired. The negative force of exhaustion seems to mentally tie one arm behind Sam's back.

## LOVE vs. NEGATIVE FORCES

Negative forces are part of every athletic contest. You cannot escape them. Some attack your mind. Others attack your body. They all try to stifle your athletic performance. One of the side-benefits that will be yours, as you learn to unleash your love for God through your athletic performance, is properly dealing with those negative forces.

John, a friend of mine, found this to be true in his wrestling performance. Although he had won a conference championship, the negative force of fear constantly tormented him. After learning how he could use his wrestling ability as an expression of his love for God, he discovered a new intensity in his performance. He said, "I can tell the difference in my wrestling already. One big area of change for me has been in the area of fear. I didn't realize until it was pointed out in your talk how great a handicap fear can be to an athletic performance. I was afraid of two things. First, I was afraid of injury. Then I was afraid of the pain that comes with a total commitment in a wrestling performance.

"The pain of fatigue really used to get to me. Because I knew from experience the reality of pain, I hesitated to give all I had. Now, instead of looking at the discomfort of pain, I look at the opportunity I have to express my love for God in my athletic performance. Yesterday my coach commented on how much he thought I had improved."

John became a "new" wrestler when he learned how to express his love for God through his wrestling.

Pain was still present in his athletic performance but it did not produce the negative force of fear. John's brain was preoccupied with expressing his love for God. A pre-occupied brain is less aware of negative forces.

## A NEW FOCAL POINT IS NEEDED

Courses in prepared childbirth are taught throughout the country. Childbearing is usually an extremely difficult event for a woman. Yet, women who apply the method taught in these classes rave about the tremendous joy they had in giving birth to their babies. What makes the difference between an experience of pain and fear and one of lessened discomfort and joy? It's an attitude as well as a method. We can learn an amazing truth about how the human brain works from the results of these classes. If you walked into a class where husbands and wives were being taught the prepared childbirth method, you would see a strange sight. You would see pregnant women slowly moving their fingers in circular motions over their abdomens while breathing in a slow and controlled manner. You would notice that these women were staring at a fixed point—usually an inanimate object in the room. The premise is that the brain can concentrate at 100% capacity on only one thing at a time. To block out the discomfort of labor, the woman concentrates on three things at the same time: 1) her focal point on the inanimate object; 2) her controlled breathing; and 3) her fingers making slow circular motions on her abdomen. Pain must register in the brain but a pre-occupied brain is less aware of it.

As we saw from John's experience, this fact is equally true in athletics. John found his fear diminished in his wrestling performance as his focal point became God. His greatest desire was to express his love for Him. The work of the Holy Spirit made that possible.

## HOW LOVE OVERCOMES NEGATIVE FORCES

In the last chapter we briefly touched upon the athletic implications of Romans 12:1. This great passage is the key to understanding HOW love conquers negative forces.

> "I urge you therefore, brethren, by the mercies of God, to present your bodies a living and holy sacrifice, acceptable to God, which is your spiritual service of worship."

The word "brethren" tells Paul was writing to fellow Christians. His phrase, "by the mercies of God" could also be rendered "because of what God accomplished for you by Christ dying on the cross." The verb "present" simply means to turn over to someone else the control of something you have. Although the word "bodies" refers to all your physical characteristics, it's important to bear in mind it also includes specifically your athletic abilities (e.g., reflex action, speed, strength, coordination, etc.). The next phrase "living and holy sacrifice" is what makes it possible for you to overcome negative forces. It is the result of your love expression. The phrase refers to you as dead to yourself (sacrifice) and alive to the control of Jesus Christ through the Holy Spirit (living). This quality in your athletic performance makes it "acceptable" to God for His purpose.

The last phrase "spiritual service of worship" also can be rendered "the logical way for you to express your love for God." Let's camp on this one for a moment. The Greek word used for "service of worship" describes any form of service that results out of a love relationship with God. It includes your athletic performance. For instance, two javelin throwers let the javelins fly with all their energy. The javelins sail through the air and land. God is pleased with one performance but not the other. Why? Motivation made the difference. One threw the javelin for his own personal glory. His only thought was about what the throw would do for himself. The other athlete threw the javelin as an expression of his love for God. He wasn't concerned for his own glory. The phrase, "service of worship" includes running the bases as well as tackling a runner. It includes dribbling a basketball downcourt as well as throwing a javelin. It includes everything you will ever do in your athletic performance. This service is a love expression to God.

If you were a shepherd in Old Testament days, it would have been logical for you to select the best lamb to give back to God as an expression of your love. Since you are an athlete, rather than an Old Testament shepherd, it isn't logical for you to offer a lamb on the altar as an expression of your love for God. You're involved in athletics, not sheep herding. But it is logical for you to offer your athletic ability on the altar of the basketball court, football field, baseball diamond, wrestling mat, etc. Your athletic abilities are a gift from God. Since you are an athlete, it is logical for you to offer the best quality of your abilities to Him as an expression of your love. That logical way for you to express your love for God is the "spiritual" way.

> "I urge and encourage you, (insert your name), because of what God accomplished for you when Jesus Christ died on the cross, to place all your athletic abilities at God's disposal throughout your athletic performance. Allow God, through the Holy Spirit, to control your attitudes and actions. This not only will be acceptable to Him, but it is the most

logical way you can express your love to God tangibly while competing."

(Athletic Paraphrase of Romans 12:1)

Here's an example of how one athlete, Tom, applied Romans 12:1 to his athletic performance. He explains his experience in overcoming negative forces during one of the biggest wrestling tournaments of the year.

"Each year there are between 35 and 50 wrestlers in your weight class so you must win a lot of preliminary matches to reach the finals. I entered the tournament with a great desire to place. More importantly, I wanted to give a total release of all that I was in performing like Jesus.

"I barely won my first match on a ride time point that was given to me after the match ended in a tie. During the match I wasn't doing so well as I had planned. All I could think of was 'Oh no! Tom, you're going to mess up again in this big tournament.' At one point when I was behind, the thought raced through my mind that I might just as well give up since I wasn't wrestling as well as I could have. But I knew that wouldn't be a total release performance and I would be a loser in God's eyes if I allowed it to control me. I decided to wrestle to the best of my ability for the rest of the match and leave the outcome to God. I ended up winning but I still knew something was keeping me from really experiencing the feeling of going all out physically, mentally and spiritually. I just didn't know what it was.

"My next match was against a guy who had pinned me when we wrestled two years earlier. We wrestled about even for the first two periods but I soon sensed that I wasn't really free. Something was keeping me from following through with my moves. I ended up losing the match 7–3.1 hoped that the man who just beat me would continue to win his matches so that I would be able to wrestle in the consolation bracket. He did. That gave me a chance to come back again later that night. I talked with my coach, explaining how I was really confused because I wasn't performing up to my potential even though I had prepared for the match and I wanted to express my love to Jesus through it. That night I won my first consolation match by a decision and my second one by a forfeit.

"After thinking about it and praying later that night, I finally realized what my problem was. I had been trying to give a total release of myself to perform like Jesus but I had taken my eyes off Him. I had been focusing my attention on the tournament and the other wrestlers in my weight class. I had been thinking about all of the matches I would have to win to earn a place. As a result, I wasn't free in my mind to give a real total release of my potential. The next day was completely different. I took my eyes off the number of matches and who my opponent would be and committed each one as a love expression to the Lord. I just took them one at a time. I was able to beat my next three opponents while at the same time experiencing a freedom to wrestle to my potential. In fact, my last match was against the same wrestler who had defeated me the night before. I won this match 5–3, even though it was only 24 hours later. I learned that I had to do the same thing Jesus did when He went to the cross. He took His eyes off the odds and simply went out to finish the task His Father called Him to do."

## NEGATIVE FORCES DEFEATED

If the only desire of the athletes in our opening examples was to express their love for God through their athletic performance, how would they have handled their negative forces?

## Example One

Offensive lineman in football seldom get the credit they deserve. On the other hand, players in more noticeable positions often get credit as a result of the lineman's work. Brad is not concerned with getting credit for his performance since his only audience is God. He takes the truth of Colossians 3:23 seriously where he is told to do his work heartily for the Lord rather than for other men. Since he has committed his line play to be an expression of his love for God, his attention is not diverted by the acclaim given one of the running backs. He feels satisfied knowing that he is doing what God has for him. He continues to contribute to the team by making it possible for another person to gain the yards.

## Example Two

Gary realizes that physical injury is the possible byproduct of any physical activity. Ten stitches around his eyes are proof. He gets away from focusing his attention on possible injury by using his performances as an expression of his love for God. He couldn't tell much of a difference at first Fear of the "sharp" elbows was still on his mind. It wasn't until he realized what Jesus endured on the cross as His expression of love for Gary that he took his eyes off himself. Now Gary mentally prepares for each practice and game by picturing himself going after rebounds as an expression of his love for God. He looks forward to the action as a result of this preparation.

## Example Three

It was relatively easy for Ted to concentrate on each golf shot as a separate expression of love for God. He discovered there was nothing he could do about someone else's score. The truth of Romans

8:28 helped him keep God's perspective on his golf game. When Ted understood that "God causes ALL THINGS to work together for good to those who love God, to those who are called according to His purpose" (Romans 8:28), he was free to concentrate only on his expression of love for God. He knew that "all things" included the performance of his opponent as well as his own performance. God's purpose is never stymied by circumstances.

## Example Four

Sam's "one arm tied behind his back" because of exhaustion was quickly untied when he set his attention back on expressing his love for God in his moves. He realized that if God desired him to defeat his opponent, God could give him the endurance no matter how tired he felt. His only responsibility was to unleash all he did have as an expression of his love. He couldn't be responsible for the strength and energy already expended on the mat. Sam was reminded by one of his Christian teammates that Jesus Christ could give him the strength and energy he needed if He should choose to do so. His mind shifted from the negative force of exhaustion to the positive task of expressing his love for God regardless of whether or not he received additional strength and energy.

Athletics take on a whole new excitement when they are simply **opportunities to express one's love for God.** The interesting by-product is overcoming negative forces that would ordinarily stifle your athletic performance.

## FOR DISCUSSION

1. Name some negative forces and explain how they can hinder your athletic performance.

2. Describe two different ways negative forces can affect your athletic performance. Give some personal example.

3. Explain how love overcomes negative forces according to Romans 12:1.

4. Explain how you *cannot* give a total release of yourself to perform like Jesus while looking at your competition.

5. Use the examples mentioned to discuss how negative forces can be used as opportunities for you to express your love for God.

**GOD IS MORE INTERESTED IN BUILDING CHARACTER THAN ANYTHING ELSE (DEFEATING YOUR OPPONENT, MAKING THE TEAM, WINNING THE LEAGUE CHAMPIONSHIP OR SETTING A RECORD).**

> "For whom He foreknew, He also predestined to become conformed to the image of His Son . . ."
>
> (Romans 8:29)

# CHAPTER 12

# THE PRAISE PERFORMANCE

The shortstop is crouched, ready to spring into action. At the crack of the bat, he races to his left and quickly scoops the ball into his glove. While on the dead run, he twists his body, cocks his arm and throws the runner out at first base. If his action had a voice, you would hear it cry out, “Praise the Lord!”

In a split second the basketball guard steals the ball and dribbles halfway down court. Then, with blinding speed and pinpoint accuracy, he passes to a teammate who drives in for an easy lay-up. If their actions had voices, they would be shouting, “Praise the Lord!”

The ball is snapped and the wide receiver begins his moves. With a hip fake and foot plant, he breaks to the right. The ball is in the air racing for its target. The wide receiver and defender lunge for it at the same time. With his fingers extended beyond what he thought was possible, the receiver grabs the ball and falls to the turf. If his action could speak, it would be shouting, “Praise the Lord!”

## PRAISE GOD WITH YOUR ATHLETIC ABILITIES

Can this actually be? Is it possible to praise the Lord with your athletic performance? A brand new excitement in performing will echo through your actions as you understand the implication Psalms 150 has for your athletic performance. Yes, it is possible to praise the Lord through the bodily motions of your athletic performance. One way to express your love for God is through praising Him. God has designed you to praise Him. For instance, your voice is a gift from God.

With it you can sing His praises. Your physical abilities are also gifts from God. With them you can express your praise of Him. What greater way could there possibly be for you, as an athlete, to unleash your love for God than through your athletic performance?

The writer of Psalms 150 puts it this way:

1 "Praise the Lord!
Praise God in His sanctuary;
Praise Him in His mighty expanse.
2 Praise Him for His mighty deeds;
Praise Him according to His excellent greatness.
3 Praise Him with trumpet sound;
Praise Him with harp and lyre.
4 Praise Him with timbrel and dancing;
Praise Him with stringed instruments and pipe.
5 Praise Him with loud cymbals;
Praise Him with resounding cymbals.
6 Let everything that has breath praise the Lord.
Praise the Lord."

## PRAISE EXPLAINED

What a tremendous psalm. It explains **where** (verse 1) **why** (verse 2) and **how** (verses 3–5) to praise God. It also explains **who** should praise Him (verse 6).

Let's define what the Bible means when we're told to praise God. The word "praise" first of all means "to shine." Then it means "to make clear." Finally, it means "to exclaim in a loud tone." That's what Psalms 150:3–5 is describing. It describes a blend of musical instruments in one great symphony of sounds. Their purpose is to **shine** forth the greatness of God. It is to focus **clearly** on Him and to **shout out** His praises in a **loud tone.** Their purpose is to **praise the Lord!**

**Where** are we to praise God? In times past, the word "sanctuary" referred primarily to the temple, but today it is understood to refer to any place where God dwells throughout His entire creation. There is no place where we are not to praise Him. You can even praise God in a ball park. There is not a locker room too smelly nor a stadium too large in which God cannot be praised. You can praise Him on the baseball diamond, on the basketball court and on the football field. You can praise God on a wrestling mat, on a golf course and on the tennis court. You are in His dwelling place no matter where you are or what you are doing. There is no place on this earth where you cannot praise the Lord!

**Why** praise God? We're to praise Him because of the mighty things He has done and for **who** He is. We applaud the man who designs and builds great skyscrapers. He deserves it. Greater applause should go to the God who created all material out of nothing but by His Word. In awe we hold the One who designed the human brain that plans and builds the skyscrapers.

Can you begin to count the stars above or give them names? God knows exactly how many stars there are for He designed and created them all. Do you know how many grains of sand are on a seashore or how many hairs are on your head? God does (Isaiah

40:12 and Matthew 10:30). Can you be in the United States and England at the same instant? God is (Psalms 139:4–8)! He deserves to be praised for who He is and what He has done.

**How** do you praise God? Psalms 150:3–5 describes three musical instruments used in praising God. They represent the three basic classes of instruments used in an orchestra—wind, stringed and percussion. Each has a distinct sound and use. Each can be made to sound good by itself, but all three blended together make the most pleasant music. They can play softly throughout or they can be blended in a series of lows and highs of melodious and rhythmic sound.

## THE "ATHLETIC ORCHESTRA"

Let's begin to think of your athletic abilities as an orchestra praising God through your athletic performance. We can even use a music orchestra as an analogy to understand how actions of the body can be used to praise God. Each of the instruments mentioned in verses 3–5 can be compared to various parts of your body. For instance, your heart can be the **trumpet** in your "athletic orchestra." The trumpet is a wind instrument. It requires energy from within to force the air through its long tube. When this is done, clear notes are sounded out for all the countryside to hear. It creates an excitement and stirs deep emotions. The same is true of your heart. The more it is called upon to supply oxygen to your muscles, the more exciting is the action of your athletic performance.

Let's say you begin an easy jog. Your heartbeat is slow and steady. There is no great excitement yet. Down the straightaway you pick up the pace. Your heart responds with a faster beat. More oxygen is pumped into your muscles. Then you turn it on.

You're racing at top speed. Your heart pounds faster and faster. Greater is the excitement. With every beat, more oxygen is carried to your tiring muscles. If your heart was a trumpet, the loud, clear sounds would resound through the entire countryside. Every good orchestra needs the trumpet. You have one built in to sound out praises to God.

The **harp and lyre** are stringed instruments. Both require a fine touch and produce a flowing melody of notes. They require the same fine touch as it takes to sink a five foot putt or shoot a free throw. Melody is required in all athletic movement. The harp and lyre, or other similar stringed instruments, are necessary in an orchestra to carry the melody. They make things flow.

In your "athletic orchestra" your eyes, ears, nose, mouth, hands and feet can be the harps and lyres. With them you create a flow of action that forms the melody of your athletic performance. A melody is simply a continuous flow of notes or sounds that blend together to make a complete song. The purpose of your hands and feet is to produce a flowing movement in your execution. Your eyes, ears, nose and mouth are finer tuned instruments that add the balance. For instance, controlled breathing (through the nose or mouth) can create a calm, if slow breaths are taken. You can add a faster tempo by breathing faster in a controlled manner. The tennis player, as he darts from sideline to sideline, can calm himself by a slower, controlled breathing. He brings the melody of his performance to a slower tempo to conserve energy. Every song of praise has both slow and soft music as well as the fast and harder tempo. Every athletic performance likewise has both a slow and fast tempo.

The **timbrel** was a percussion instrument. It added rhythm to the symphony of sounds. The timbrel, similar to the instrument we know as the tambourine, had a parchment covering either a round or square frame. Little bells or pieces of brass were fastened in the rim. It sounded like a drum with bells when hit with the hand. The timbrel accentuated feelings and emotions in the melody.

Percussion instruments, such as the timbrel, can be compared to your legs, arms and back. They add rhythm that flows through the melody. Percussion instruments sound with a suddenness. They emphasize a beat. To some extent they seem to explode. Wind instruments, like the trumpet, can create excitement. But the percussion instruments **are** excitement.

Your legs, arms and back can be regarded as the percussion instruments in your "athletic orchestra." A linebacker moves quickly to his left. He plants his left foot and darts powerfully to meet the oncharging running back.

Picture in slow motion his powerful legs and lower back driving into the ball carrier while his arms wrap around him with great sounds of percussion. Contact and the loud "clanging of cymbals" is heard throughout the stadium.

Every orchestra must have a director to oversee the perfect blending of music. Without total allegiance to that director, each instrument in an orchestra would play its own music. The results would be harsh and not pleasing to the ear. A good director causes a perfect blending of rhythm and percussion throughout the music to accentuate the melody.

The director in your "athletic orchestra" is your brain. Impulses are sent from it to each instrument of your body, calling for a perfect blend of melody, rhythm and percussion in praise to God. Now that we have considered how your body can be an "athletic orchestra," let's think through some ideas on praising God in this athletic paraphrase of several Bible passages.

> Praise the Lord . . . Let your thoughts and actions shine forth to reflect the grandeur of God. Be aware of who God is throughout your body and mind. Shout the greatness of God in your every move.
>
> Praise God in the locker room and shower. Praise Him throughout each practice session and competition. Praise Him at the training table and in the classroom. Everywhere you are, Praise the Lord.[1]
>
> Praise Him for what He has done. Celebrate the victory you have through Jesus on the cross. He has selected you for His family.[2]
>
> Let your mind and body sing a new song about His greatness![3] He knows when you go to sleep and when you awake. He understands every thought you have.[4] Before you speak a word He knows what it will be.[5] He is everywhere at the same time. In a flash you can go to the depths of the sea and He will greet you. You can soar to the highest of the heavens and He is already there. In the midst of darkness He sees as though it were the brightest day.[6] He has formed you with a perfect design to accomplish His purpose. Before you were even in your mother's womb, He designed your life. He knows the events of your life before they even happen. He designed them. His thoughts of you are more plentiful than sand on all the seashores.[7]

He owns the cattle on a thousand hills. Everything that moves in the fields are His.[8] Look at the stars above. He knows their exact number and calls each by name. Because of His greatness, not one of them is missing.[9]

Let your mind be absorbed with His greatness. Let your body resound to His majesty. For the Everlasting God, the Creator of all this earth, does not tire or grow weary. He pours His strength to you. To those who lack, He increases their power.[10]

## PRAISE GOD THROUGH YOUR ATHLETIC PERFORMANCE

Let the energy flow from within, reflecting His greatness. Praise Him through your stamina. Let the melody of your song before Him be seen in the quickness of your reflexes and dexterity of your fingers. Praise God through the rhythm of your strides. Shout His praise with perfect timing. Shout praises to the Lord with every fiber in your body.

Let His presence shine forth through you. Reflect His pureness through your athletic performance. With a performance constantly in rhythm with the presence of God, let it build for a great "Praise the Lord." Sing forth your praise through your speed, quickness, dexterity, strength, stamina and explosiveness. Let your performance sing praises to God. Shout it out with all the energy within you! "Let everything that has breath praise the Lord. Praise the Lord" (Psalms 150:6)!!

The Lord desires our praise of Him in whatever we do. It is not limited to the choir loft in a church service, nor is it limited to an expression through your athletic performance. Your praise of God is to flow through you in whatever you are doing.

As you walk and talk, praise Him through your attitudes, thoughts and actions. Praise the Lord as you select food to eat. Praise Him as you face interruptions to a well-planned schedule. Reflect His presence. Praise the Lord in your selection of newspaper articles, magazines and books to read. Praise the Lord as you select which television programs to watch. Let your understanding of others honor God as you are aware of His presence. You are His servant. Praise Him with all that you are in whatever you are doing.

It's interesting that each of the instruments in Psalms 150 is an instrument of joy. Each gave clear, bright sounds and created an aura of joy (gladness). You are designed for the same purpose. You can use your legs, arms, hands, eyes, ears and all parts of your body to express your praise of God. You can unleash your love for God in a Praise Performance.

## BIBLICAL REFERENCES

1. Psalms 150:1
2. Psalms 150:2
3. Psalms 149:1
4. Psalms 139:2
5. Psalms 139:4
6. Psalms 139:7–12
7. Psalms 139:13–18
8. Psalms 50:10–11
9. Isaiah 40:26
10. Isaiah 40:28–29

## FOR DISCUSSION

1. How does your body relate to the musical instruments of an orchestra in praising God through your athletic performance?

2. How is it possible to praise the Lord with your athletic performance?

## CHAPTER 13

# CHARACTERISTICS AND RESULTS OF A PRAISE PERFORMANCE

In the last chapter we caught a glimpse of how you can praise God through your athletic performance. The Praise Performance is probably an entirely new athletic concept for you. In the Praise Performance you have a different goal and motivation than you normally would in your athletic performances. Your only goal is to have the attitudes, thoughts and actions of Jesus Christ. Your mind is completely controlled by the Holy Spirit, who is conforming you to the image of Christ. You have God's perspective on winning. You are more concerned about totally releasing yourself toward presenting Jesus Christ than you are with the final score. Your only motivation is to express your love for God. The Praise Performance perfectly blends all the biblical principles explained in this handbook.

One of the interesting athletic side benefits, resulting from practicing the Praise Performance, is a rhythm that flows through your mind, keeping you consistently primed for a maximum performance. Staleness in any athletic performance begins with the mind. There is no room for staleness in a mind praising God for who He is and what He has done. Because this is a new way of competing, we're going to take a look at some characteristics and results of such a performance in this chapter before actually studying how to develop it in the following chapter.

## CHARACTERISTIC NUMBER ONE

**The focus of what you are thinking and doing throughout your athletic performance is on God.** You are not bothered by varying circumstances such as temperature, score, aches, opposing team, etc. These circumstances are simply new opportunities for you to praise God through your athletic performance. You are no longer comparing yourself with performances of the past or dreams of the future. You are not overly concerned about the outcome of the contest. Your **only** focus throughout the performance is on God. Your only desire throughout your performance is to praise Him for who He is and what He has done.

## CHARACTERISTIC NUMBER TWO

**You prepare for your Praise Performance before it begins.** Although we will examine preparation more closely in the next chapter, it is important enough to mention as one of the five characteristics of a Praise Performance. Such preparation takes place in your mind. This characteristic is similar to the first one in that your attention is focusing on God. It is different only in that it takes place **before** actual competition begins. Before your athletic event, teammates in the locker room might be noisily stirring around you. However, your thoughts are focused on who God is and the great things He has done. By using the steps in the next chapter to develop a Praise Performance, you will see how your mind blends God's Word with Christian music.

## CHARACTERISTIC NUMBER THREE

**The melody and rhythm that began in your mind accentuate your athletic skills in practice and competition.** Your mind and body blend together with a fresh excitement as you run, jump, tackle, throw or whatever it is you do in your athletic performance. The height of your jump can be likened to a clashing of cymbals. The crispness of your throws emphasize your praise of God.

## CHARACTERISTIC NUMBER FOUR

**You have a great desire to cooperate with your teammates.** In your praise of God, you say and do things for the good of your teammates. Your attitudes, words and actions can lift the spirit of your entire team. We'll see how important this is in the chapter on *The Perfect Team Spirit.* The time might come when you will have an entire team participating in a Praise Performance of God. It begins with you.

## CHARACTERISTIC NUMBER FIVE

**You see each competition as a new opportunity to praise God with your attitudes and actions.** Your opponent is not a personal enemy. He might even be a fellow Christian. Your athletic strategy, however, is geared to defeat him in the score. But your primary purpose, as you strategically point to defeat him, is to praise God with your attitudes and actions. Strategy is an important part of preparing for competition. If a baseball hitter's strength is a high fastball, you will want to throw him breaking pitches or keep the ball low and away. If the football running back has blazing speed to the outside, you will want to turn him in whenever he carries the football. If the one you are guarding in basketball is a deadly shot at the range of ten feet, you will want to keep him moving away from his favorite position on the court. Once your strategy has been determined, you can generate your attention to praising God with attitudes and actions that represent Jesus Christ.

Of course, you will make strategy changes during the competition. But once these are made, your attention is again focused on praising God through your attitudes and actions. Your opponent simply provides you with different types of opportunities to reflect your praise of God through your athletic performance. For instance, he might be working a strategy against you that prompts you to alter yours. He might be overly aggressive in his actions against you. You have an opportunity to endure his tactics with the attitude of Jesus as you're empowered by the Holy Spirit. But your attitude and actions are more than simply putting up with his tactics. Your attitudes and actions are a positive expression of your praise of God.

A Praise Performance contains all five characteristics. You don't need to keep checking to see if they're all present. They will be if you prepare and carry out the how-to's of the next chapter.

The first part of this chapter has given you an idea of what will happen during a Praise Performance. Now let's take a look at four results of such an experience.

## RESULT NUMBER ONE

Praising God in everything you do, including your athletic performance, **prepares you for an eternity of praising God!** Revelation 4:9–11 describes what our role with God in eternity will be like:

> "And when the living creatures [all of nature] give glory and honor and thanks to Him [God] who sits on the throne, to Him who lives forever and ever, the twenty-four elders [all Christians including you] will fall down before the throne saying, 'Worthy art Thou, our Lord and our God, to receive glory and

honor and power; for Thou didst create all things, and because of Thy will they existed, and were created.' "

Your role throughout all eternity is to praise God and do what pleases Him. Just think, your athletics can be used to help prepare you for that role.

## RESULT NUMBER TWO

**Praising God in your athletic performance results in a more personal relationship with Him throughout every area of your life.** Your athletic performance will no longer be isolated from the rest of your Christian life. Your praise of God will be consistent throughout all areas of your life—including your athletic performance. For instance, in athletic competition you praise God through your attitudes and actions just as you do in the classroom or in your home.

## RESULT NUMBER THREE

**Praising God in everything you do enables you to enjoy victory and go through defeat with equal stability.** You praise God in **all** situations, knowing that His purpose is **always** brought about for those who love Him and are called according to His purpose (Romans 8:28).

His purpose is for you to think and perform in the same manner as Jesus Christ as the Holy Spirit conforms you to Christ's likeness. God works all things in your life, including defeats and victories, into a perfect plan to draw recognition to Himself. Since your attention is on God and your purpose is to praise Him, you won't be shaken by a defeat or *over*-elated by a victory. Disappointment is the result of failing to achieve your goal. If your goal is to defeat your opponent, you will be greatly disappointed if you fail. However, if your goal is to think and act like Jesus, empowered by the Holy Spirit, you will not have such a wide range of emotions from victory to defeat. You can fully praise God on the short end of a 90–60 score in basketball just as you can in receiving a gold medal at the Olympic Games.

## RESULT NUMBER FOUR

**Praising God In everything you do enables your athletic ability to be maximized in each practice and competition.** In most situations, your thoughts stifle your athletic performance more than your physical actions. Your mind was designed by God to express your praise of Him. Your body was designed by God to express that praise in action. In your performance, as you praise God both mentally and physically, you will be doing the very thing for which you were designed. By performing the way you were designed, your athletic ability is developed to the maximum potential.

One basketball player, after he was taught some basics of the Praise Performance, summed it up well when he said, "I can really praise God with my body. The way I think, the way I perform, the way I treat my opponent and the people in the stands are all part of it."

We're ready now, in the next chapter, to look at how you can make this Praise Performance real in your athletic performance as an expression of your love for God.

## FOR DISCUSSION

1. What are five characteristics of a praise performance and how do they individually apply to your athletic performance?

2. Why should there be no staleness in your mind during your athletic performance? If it should occur, how do you deal with it?

3. Discuss how the four results of a praise performance can become a reality in your athletic performance.

## CHAPTER 14

# DEVELOPING THE PRAISE PERFORMANCE

As an athlete, you can praise the Lord through your athletic performance.

> "Let *everything* that has breath praise the Lord. Praise the Lord!"
>
> (Psalms 150:6)

If you have breath, you can praise the Lord. You are not limited to praising Him only through singing or playing a musical instrument. You can praise Him with your athletic abilities.

A friend of mine experienced the truth of the above psalm in his weightlifting training. Each repetition he performed was an opportunity to express his praise of God. This sounds so contradictory to our natural way of training and competition, doesn't it? It is! Our natural way is not God's way. When competing God's way, your alertness to your opponent or score is only for the purpose of planning strategy. Your purpose for competition is to express your praise of God as the Holy Spirit conforms you to the likeness of Jesus Christ. The end result of such a performance accomplishes God's purpose for it according to Romans 8:28–29. My friend mentally prepared to make each practice session an experience of worshipping God. He practiced the steps of developing the Praise Performance that you'll read in this chapter and experienced the following three benefits as a result of his diligent preparation.

1. He continued his close fellowship with God throughout his entire training session. His fellowship was not postponed for three hours because of his workout.

2. He consistently had more effective training sessions since his mind was focused on God and not the heaviness of the weights.

3. He looked forward to his workouts with a new excitement because they were opportunities to worship and praise God with his athletic abilities.

In this chapter you'll see how to develop a Praise Performance. These steps for developing your Praise Performance are **suggestions** only and in no way should be taken to be the only way.

## HERE'S WHAT YOU DO WHEN YOU PRAISE GOD

1. You consciously express your love to God for who He is and what He has done.

2. You consciously have attitudes, thoughts and actions that are pleasing to God.

## YOUR MIND CONTROLS YOUR ACTIONS

Try this experiment to find out how greatly your mind influences the actions of your body.

1. Draw fifteen circles, each the size of a penny, on a piece of paper. Be sure to place them in the pyramid order shown in this drawing.

2. Number each of the circles so they correspond to the numbers in the drawing.

3. With fifteen pennies in your hand, find the circle numbered "1" and place a penny on it. Continue with the second penny on circle #2. Finish placing all the pennies in the circles in numerical order up to #15, one at a time.

4. Remove the pennies and repeat several times.

5. When you have placed them as fast as you can, time yourself.

6. Now, add this one variation as you time yourself again. As you place the pennies in the proper circles, count backwards aloud as fast as you can, from **thirty** to one. Your counting backwards must be fast, accurate and without any hesitating. Your concentration must be on the counting. Time yourself to see how fast you're able to place the pennies on the circles in numerical order while counting backwards.

Surprised at the difference in times? Most likely your time with the variation was slower than without it.

This demonstrates how your mind does influence the actions of your body. Your mind can focus at a 100% capacity on only one thing at a time. Since this is true, what occupies your mind during your athletic performance is extremely important. Your mind controls the purpose for your actions. For instance, if you are thirsty, the desire for liquid refreshment registers in your mind. In turn, the message is sent to the rest of your body to take action. You walk to the kitchen, fill a glass with water and drink it. Your body did not automatically do that. It did so only because your mind gave it directions. This brings us to a very important truth of the Praise Performance. Your athletic abilities will express your praise of God, registering in your mind, through your athletic performance. A mind controlled by the Holy Spirit produces actions controlled by the Holy Spirit. According to Psalms 150:6, God desires you to praise Him. "Let everything that has breath, praise the Lord. Praise the Lord!"

## DEVELOPING THE PRAISE PERFORMANCE

We saw in chapter four that we experience the Holy Spirit at work in us most effectively when our mind is focused on a portion of God's Word. Therefore, a true Praise Performance is one that is an expression of your response to that portion of God's word in your mind. As you will see, this expression is highlighted with actual Christian music such as "The Hallelujah Chorus," "How Great Thou Art," "Alleluia," etc. This combination of God's Word and music is blended together in your mind and released through your athletic performance. For instance, as you run the mile, you might be meditating on the return of Jesus for His Church. The "Hallelujah Chorus" would be ideal to bring emphasis to your meditation. Your stride will express your praise of God for this great future event.

## PREPARATION FOR THE PRAISE PERFORMANCE

Preparation for the Praise Performance involves your mind (the director of your "athletic orchestra") blending together three separate ingredients—God's Word, Christian music and a mental picture of your athletic performance.

## INGREDIENT NUMBER ONE—GOD'S WORD

The Bible explains who God is and what He has done. God is the **object** of your Praise Performance. King David danced in the streets out of gratitude to God when the Ark was recovered from the enemy (II Samuel 6:14). You, too, can reflect your thankfulness to God through your physical action.

The purpose of the Praise Performance is to express your love and gratitude to God for who He is and what He has done. It is not to beat your opponent. God is the center of your athletic performance. To know who God is and what He has done, you must spend time with Him through His Word. (See a list of Bible passages at the end of this chapter for suggested focal points for your praise.)

## INGREDIENT NUMBER TWO—CHRISTIAN MUSIC

Christian music is the agent that blends God's Word with your athletic performance in this method of developing a Praise Performance. In chapter twelve we looked at the analogy of your body as an "athletic orchestra." The music your "athletic orchestra" expresses in the Praise Performance is actual Christian music you have heard on recordings. It must be appropriate music for both the portion of God's Word and your particular athletic event. Here are some guidelines in choosing the kind of music that will be expressed in your "athletic orchestra."

1. Select only music that is honoring to God. Some so-called "Christian" music is nothing more than the beat of the world with "spiritual" words. Most music that stirs up natural passions in yourself is not honoring to God. The music you select should draw your attention to the person and works of God.

2. Select only music that can highlight the particular portion of God's Word upon which your mind is focused. For instance, if you were focusing your attention upon the creation, you would not want music that is gentle and soft with no climax. You would want music that builds to great peaks with perhaps the clashing of cymbals. Creation is expressive and awesome. The music that represents it must also be expressive and awesome. If your attention is focused upon the crucifixion, you would want music that is dramatic in nature. It would carry in it the sounds of agony, and then perhaps build to a clashing of cymbals, denoting the death of Christ. The music you select must emphasize and highlight the portion of God's Word you have in your mind.

3. Select only music that is appropriate for your athletic event. Here are some thoughts in choosing music for various sports. If your sport isn't listed, you can get an idea of how to select music from the following examples:

*Baseball* is a sport that is quiet for awhile, then speeds up quickly. The music should have an easy flowing melody with an obvious rhythm. The rhythm keeps your body ready for those quick explosions of energy.

*Basketball* is a steady flow of action with frequent, sudden sprints. You might want music that has many highs and lows to emphasize this action.

*Football* is dramatic and heavily accented in action. You might select music that has drums building to a peak since football is a contact sport. The clashing of cymbals would be ideal as long as they emphasize your focal point on God's Word.

*Golf* is a sport that requires an easy flowing rhythm throughout your entire body. This music should have an easy flowing melody with light accents. You want to time hitting the ball on one of the light accents.

*Tennis* is a flowing sport. It is constant, easy movements with light accents. The music you choose should reflect that action. It should have an easy flowing melody with the proper amount of rhythm to emphasize hitting the ball.

*Wrestling* is either constant movement or planning for movement. The music should have a melody and rhythm that blend toward various dramatic points.

Evaluate the type of physical movements involved in your sport. Then select music that will emphasize those physical movements as well as highlight the portion of God's Word in your mind.

In preparation for a Praise Performance, it's helpful to listen to Christian music on a tape recorder or phonograph. Listen to it several times until it is strongly imprinted in your mind. Each time you listen, picture in your mind the portion of the Bible upon which you are focusing your attention. This is a form of meditation. God desires for you to meditate upon His Word. Through meditation His Word becomes an integral part of you.

> "But his delight is in the law of the Lord, And in His law he **meditates** day and night."
> (Psalms 1:2)

Once your mind has the music flowing through it, giving emphasis to the particular portion of God's Word, you are ready to mentally adapt it to your physical performance.

## INGREDIENT NUMBER THREE—PICTURING YOUR ATHLETIC PERFORMANCE

Mentally picture what actions you take during your performance. If you are a running back in football, picture running the ball on various plays. You will want to see yourself sidestep and twist as you break tackles. Make this an accurate picture of what can actually happen. Once you have run this through your mind a few times, do it several more times as the music and God's Word flow through your mind. This requires much practice. If you need to use the tape recorder or phonograph again, do so. You want to blend God's Word with the music while you simply picture going through the motions of your athletic performance. Practice to the point where you sense the flow of music highlighting God's Word as you picture your physical actions. Your body is an "athletic orchestra" expressing music through timing, coordination, speed and power.

Remember, your body simply carries out instructions given it by your mind. If your mind is truly praising God, in response to the portion of God's Word upon which you are focusing, then your actions will express your praise of God. The music represents both God's Word and your athletic performance. It is the agent that blends the two together. When you have prepared for the Praise Performance, you are ready to experience it.

## THE PRAISE PERFORMANCE

1. Warm up. When the various musicians in an orchestra come together, it takes them several minutes to warm up properly. They don't suddenly begin playing beautiful notes of music. They need to make sure their instruments are properly tuned. The same is true of you in preparation for your athletic performance. Take time to "tune" your athletic abilities so they will respond with maximum efficiency to the amount of stress placed upon them. You want your abilities to respond in clear notes of praise. During this warm-up period, practice moving your body as an expression of praise to God. As you do this, your mind should still be focused on the portion of God's Word and the music flowing through it. Your athletic performance is a combination of the physical and the mental. Both dimensions must be warmed up properly for the best results. This is also the proper time to "warm-up" your spiritual dimension. Be sure you are totally controlled by the Holy Spirit. Your performance will be one of expressing what you have in your mind—your praise of God. You can only praise God when you're controlled by the Holy Spirit.

2. During competition, remind yourself that each situation, regardless of its difficulty, is an opportunity to express your praise of God. That's the purpose of your competition as the Holy Spirit conforms you to the likeness of Jesus.

3. Stay alert to the flow of Christian music through your mind as it draws your attention to a portion of God's Word This is a conscious effort. If your mind wanders for a few minutes, you can consciously focus it back on your purpose in the Praise Performance. Remember, the Praise Performance is a Spirit-controlled performance. Therefore, it is a

conscious performance. Our sub-conscious tendencies are seldom those of the Lord. The more you practice this, the more a part of you it will become. But, it will always be a conscious effort on your part to keep your mind focused on the right things.

## CAUTIONS

1. Don't try to put rhythm into your athletic performance without properly preparing. Rhythm that doesn't flow from your mind is counterfeit. It will be there as a result of having your mind focused on God's Word and the appropriate music.

2. Be patient in practicing the Praise Performance. It will take time for this to become the way you perform as an athlete.

3. Don't limit the Praise Performance to your athletics. God desires our praise in everything we do. Your athletic performance is the training center to praise God in every area of your life.

## FOCAL POINTS

The following Bible passages are suggested as focal points for your praise. This list contains only a few of the many great passages in the Bible that tell us who God is and what He has done. It's a good starting point. You'll find more on your own as you explore the riches of God's Word. As you focus your mind on one passage each day, shout out your praise of God in all that you do.

> "Let everything that has breath praise the Lord. Praise the Lord!"
>
> (Psalms 150:6)

1 Chronicles 16:29–33

Nehemiah 9:6

Job 26:7–14

Job 37:1–13

Job 38:1–18

Job 38:25–41

Job 39:19–25

Job 39:26–30

Psalms 33:8–9

Psalms 40:5

Psalms 75:1

Psalms 86:8

Psalms 89:9, 11–12

Psalms 104

Isaiah 44:23

Isaiah 55:12

Jeremiah 32:17

1 Corinthians 15:51–57

Colossians 1:16–17

## FOR DISCUSSION

1. What two things are involved in praising God through your athletic performance?

2. What is essential in developing a Praise Performance?

3. Explain the purpose of the Praise Performance.

4. Explain the three separate ingredients your mind blends together in preparation for a Praise Performance.

5. What are some Bible passages you have found to be helpful in your athletic Praise Performance? Discuss why they are relevant.

## CHAPTER 15

# PERFECTION THROUGH ISOLATION

One of the most costly errors in baseball history was committed on October 5, 1941. It was in the fourth game of the World Series between the New York Yankees and the Brooklyn Dodgers. Mickey Owen, the Dodger's catcher, was the "culprit" according to newspaper reports. The New York Yankees were at bat in the top of the ninth inning, trailing 4–3. Hugh Casey, Brooklyn's ace relief hurler, was in complete control of the game. The first two men he faced in the ninth inning weakly grounded out. Tommy Henrich, one of the Yankee's feared hitters, came to bat. He had gone hitless in the game and Casey worked the count to 3 balls and 2 strikes against him. Then, Casey uncorked his best curve ball of the day. It actually would have been ball four, but it fooled Henrich completely. He swung and missed for the third strike which should have ended the game. The problem was it also fooled Casey's catcher, Mickey Owen. The ball got by him and Henrich raced safely to first base. Unbelievably, the Yankees went on to score four runs and win the game.

Most newspaper reports of the incident declared Owen to be the man responsible for the surge of Yankee runs by opening the door with his error. There is no doubt he did make a physical error. But, in most athletic contests, it is **not** the physical errors that will hurt you. It is the affect they have on your mental attitude. To illustrate this point, let's analyze what happened following Mickey Owen's error.

Brooklyn's manage Leo Durocher, stormed to the plate in a loud protest that Henrich had interferred with Owens as he went to retrieve the ball. The protest was not considered by the umpire. However, when Durocher returned to the dugout, he was in a disturbed and frustrated mood. In the events that followed, Durocher did not demonstrate good baseball strategy. He did not make the proven and accepted percentage moves for which the situations called.

For example, Joe Dimaggio followed Henrich with a single to left field. Two men were now on base with Charlie Keller coming to bat. Keller was another of the Yankee's top hitters and already had three hits for the day. He was a left-handed hitter, while Casey was a right-handed pitcher. Durocher had a left-handed pitcher warming up in the bull-pen but did not call him in to face Keller. Statistically, left-handed pitchers have done better against left-handed hitters in comparison to how right-handed pitchers have fared. Keller, although down by a 0–2 count, blasted an extra base hit off Casey, scoring both Henrich and DiMaggio. Still Durocher kept Casey in the game. Before the inning was over, Casey had faced six additional hitters after Henrich had "struck out."

Most ardent baseball observers now agree that, although Owen's error did give the Yankees new life, it was not the game's deciding factor. Hugh Casey had been in complete command of the Yankees since the fifth inning when he entered the game. All of a sudden he couldn't get anyone out. Why? He had the same physical abilities as he had when he delivered his curve ball to Henrich. Ardent baseball observers point out two possible explanations to the barage of runs that followed. This "turning point" of the game might have brought about a greater concentrated effort by the Yankees who, until then, might have considered the game lost. On the other hand, Casey might have been shaken since he most likely thought the game should already be over. It might have been a combination of the two. Then, we have the statistically unsound strategy of Durocher when he left Casey in to pitch to six additional hitters—four of whom were among the greatest sluggers in baseball, two of which were left-handed hitters.

So-called "turning points" of a game do not alter the physical abilities of those on the playing field. All the competitors have the same abilities as before the "turning point." The difference is the mental attitude of the players. Your mental dimension controls your physical dimension. We'll now see how your spiritual dimension can give a stabilizing effect to your mental dimension which, in turn, controls your physical ability.

## BIBLICAL PREMISE FOR ISOLATION

One of the concepts God imparts to us through the apostle Paul is the concept of **isolation.** In this concept, you isolate the past from your mind and totally concentrate on your goal. Paul totally concentrated on his goal. Like ours, Paul's goal was to become conformed to the likeness of Jesus. He wrote:

> "Brethren, I do not regard myself as having laid hold of it [sinless perfection] yet, but one thing I do: **forgetting what lies behind and reaching forward to what lies ahead, I press toward the goal** [complete conformity to the likeness of Christ ] for the prize of the upward call of God in Christ Jesus."
>
> (Philippians 3:13–14)

## "TURNING POINTS" ONLY AFFECT MENTAL ATTITUDE

The reason certain events in an athletic contest become known as "turning points" is because they can have such a devastating affect on your mental attitude. They are remembered. Your thinking becomes different than before the "turning point." For instance, in a tennis match the set score is two games to one in favor of your opponent. In the fourth game he smashes a ball toward center net. The ball hits the top of the net and barely drops on your side. It's impossible for you to reach the ball. He wins the game. But, more important, instead of the set being tied two games to two, it is now three games to one. You're down two games. If you develop a defeated attitude such as, "I'll never catch him now," it can be said that his dribbled shot was the "turning point" in your set.

Let's take a look at what happens to a football running back who constantly gets "buried" by No. 88 every time he attempts to carry the ball around right end. It has happened five times already. The same play is called again. What does he picture in his mind? The five previous catastrophies. As he takes the hand-off, his eyes never leave the fast-approaching No. 88.

Instead of driving full speed ahead, the running back slows his pace to brace himself against "burial" number six.

Your natural tendency is to allow past negative experiences to influence your current action. Yet, the apostle Paul had a different way of dealing with the past. He left it completely *in the past.* Paul's only goal was to be conformed to the likeness of Jesus Christ through the work of the Holy Spirit. But Paul realized he had not yet reached the 100% conformity to

Christ 100% of the time. Did he sit around and mope about it? Of course he didn't. The word he uses for "forgetting" in Philippians 3:13–14, means he **totally** forgot. The event was no longer in his conscious mind. As far as he was concerned, it was over and **behind** him. Kenneth Wuest, in his Word Studies in the Greek New Testament, says Paul used an illustration of a Greek runner. The athlete is running with all his might and is not concerned with his opponents who are behind him. He has completely forgotten them. He doesn't allow their footsteps, near or far, to detract him from what he is doing.

## HOW TO ISOLATE

How do you completely forget about an error or a strikeout? How do you completely forget about the fumble that gave the other team good field position in football? How do you completely forget about the height of the opposing basketball team? How do you completely forget about how badly you were beaten by your opponent the last time you met?

You do it the same way the apostle Paul did. He **reached "forward to what lies ahead!"** His words, "reaching forward" are an athletic term that has the athlete focusing his full attention on a specific goal. As he does this with all his conscious effort, his physical abilities are drawn to that goal. For instance, as the Greek runner is running toward the finish line, his eyes are focused sharply on the cord streched across the track. All he can think about is getting there as quickly as his abilities will carry him. He's not distracted. His eyes never move from their focal point on the finish line. The athlete reaches forward, following the focus of his eyes.

Then, in Paul's next words, he told of the concentrated effort he used to reach his goal. He wrote, "I press on toward the goal . . ." The word "press" actually means to pursue—to actively go after something. It reveals the intensity with which Paul reached toward his goal. The word "toward" has the connotation of bearing down upon the goal. Paul constantly pursued his goal, bearing down upon it with his total energy. His only life goal was to become Christ-like.

Each situation in your athletic performance is an opportunity for you to become Christ-like as you allow the Holy Spirit to produce the attitudes, thoughts and actions of Jesus Christ through you. Your focus of attention is to be only on conforming to the likeness of Jesus in each situation.

But you will not automatically forget about such experiences by just saying, "I won't think about it anymore." Paul took the positive approach. He kept an experience from having a negative impact on his mental attitude by positively focusing his attention on his goal. It was a DELIBERATE, positive action.

**ISOLATION IN PRACTICE**

Your mind can only focus at 100% of its capacity on one thing at a time. The more you concentrate on allowing the Holy Spirit to represent Jesus Christ in your attitudes, thoughts and actions, the less influence a person or past performance will have on your mind. For instance, let's say you're a golfer. You just drove the ball in good position down the middle of the fairway. You're natural attitude is great. But, on the next shot, using a seven iron, you dub the ball barely forty yards. Now, your natural attitude isn't so good, is it? You're disappointed with yourself. You tighten a little on the next shot because you're still thinking about the missed shot with the seven iron.

How would you handle this situation using the concept of **isolation?** After your good drive, you would prepare for the seven iron shot by thinking your approach and execution of it are opportunities for you to totally represent Jesus Christ. The Holy Spirit causes your mind to focus on portions of God's Word that keep your concentration on the task at hand. (You'll find some suggestions in Appendix V.) You see the seven iron shot as an opportunity to praise God with your athletic skills. While having this thought, you dub the seven iron shot. **You continue practicing isolation following a failure, just as you do following a success.** The first thing you do is learn from whatever mistake you committed. If your inside elbow was away from your body, you'll want to correct that. Once you learn from the bad shot, you focus your attention completely on approaching the next shot. You concentrate on seeing it as an opportunity to represent Jesus Christ. Your next shot is an opportunity for you to praise God as the Holy Spirit conforms you to the likeness of Jesus Christ.

The attitude of disappointment comes only when you fail to reach your goal. By successfully practicing this concept of isolation, you will never be disappointed in the game situation since you will always be pursuing the one goal of Chirst-likeness.

You'll notice, from the golfing illustration, that **you practice isolation following every shot, whether good or bad.** The same is true of every sport. In some sports, such as basketball, water polo, wrestling, etc., you have less time to think about the past. Yet, you can still positively focus your attention on conforming to the likeness of Jesus Christ throughout the contest.

If Hugh Casey and Leo Durocher had successfully isolated Mickey Owen's error, would the result of the fourth game in the 1941 World Series have been different? We can only surmise it would have been different. However, the concept of isolation described in this chapter can only be successfully applied by the Christian athlete. It deals with our focal point being Jesus Christ. Our only goal is to become conformed to His likeness in everything we do. This draws out our maximum potential. No other goal is worthy of total allegiance. It is your total allegiance to this goal that causes you to fully concentrate on the present.

## FOR DISCUSSION

1. Explain why "turning points" are usually mental and not physical.

2. What is the concept of isolation and how are you to apply this to your athletic performance?

3. Your mind can only focus at 100% of its capacity on one thing at a time. Relate this to the concept of isolation in your athletic performance.

4. Explain how this has helped you in your athletic performance.

**THE CHRISTIAN LIFE (INCLUDING YOUR ATHLETIC PERFORMANCE) IS A CONSCIOUS EFFORT TO RELY ON THE HOLY SPIRIT TO CONTROL YOUR LIFE.**

"... be filled [controlled] with the Spirit ..."
(Ephesians 5:18)

# CHAPTER 16

# PERFECTION THROUGH "SET-BACKS"

The possibility of "athletic set-backs" strikes fear in the minds of most athletes. You train long and hard for a particular competition only to have an injury, poor grades, illness or some other circumstance deprive you of the opportunity to compete.

What sort of attitude would you have if you suffered an injury that could keep you out for the rest of the season?

You would feel frustration, wouldn't you? You've suffered a "set-back." An "athletic set-back" is any situation you experience that **hinders** your development as an athlete. By looking at situations from God's perspective, we'll see those that ordinarily would be called "athletic set-backs" do not have to be set-backs at all.

God's perspective on "set-backs" is always different than our first natural reaction to them. It's important to remember Jesus never promised a life free from difficult situations. He did promise He would be more than sufficient to see us through any difficulty.

> "These things I have spoken to you, that in Me you may have **peace.** In the world you have tribulation [e.g., physical injury, breakdown of communication, defeat, etc.], but take courage; I have overcome the world."
>
> (John 16:33)

The word "peace" has the connotation of **rest.** It refers to the **absence of inner tension.** It's interesting to note that Jesus used this word "peace" in the same verse as the word "tribulation." To have "tribulation" means to have **pressure and distress.** As you can see, "peace" and "tribulation" have opposite meanings. Jesus spoke about a person having no tension in the midst of a tension-packed situation!

Whether or not you have "peace" in "tribulation" depends on your perspective. For instance, a football player on a west coast team had always dreamed of playing in the Rose Bowl. He earned a starting role as an offensive tackle on what was rated the No. 1 team in the country. It looked as though his dream would come true. Then it happened. A knee injury, suffered in a non-conference game, required surgery. He was out for the remainder of the season. This football lineman had one of two ways to view his difficult situation. He could view it from his own perspective and see the injury as a hindrance to a possible Rose Bowl appearance and future professional career. On the other hand, he could view it from God's perspective and see the injury as an opportunity to trust God. When asked about his injury he said, "As a football player, I felt the worst thing that could happen to me would be to get hurt. But this year that's what happened. And yet, because of my relationship with Christ, I see this as a **steppingstone** to becoming a stronger person, rather than as a tragedy." His teammates noticed his attitude and, as a result, several wanted to learn more about Jesus Christ.

The Christian athlete is **not immune** from experiencing situations that could be termed "athletic setbacks." However, he can be empowered by the Holy Spirit to deal with them. In fact, God has given us instructions on what we should do when facing difficult situations.

> "Consider it all joy, my brethren, when you encounter various trials, knowing that the testing of your faith produces endurance. And let endurance have its perfect result, that you may be **perfect** and **complete,** lacking in nothing"
>
> (James 1:2–4)

The word "consider" implies **viewing** something a certain way in your mind. The word "trials" refers to anything that puts your trust in Jesus to the test. It can be an emotional disturbance, a family crisis, a break-up with your girlfriend, etc. It also includes every situation that could be termed an "athletic set-back."

When James used the word "consider" he wanted us to view each difficult situation in a specific manner. How? He wanted us to view such "set-backs" with **joy.** The word "joy" doesn't refer to happiness.

It refers to gladness. What's the difference? Happiness is based on circumstances. If the circumstances, such as an undefeated season, no injuries, good statistics, etc., are favorable, you're happy. If they're not, you're unhappy. However, gladness is an **attitude!** It has nothing to do with your circumstances.

You might be thinking, "Wait a minute. It isn't easy to be glad when you've just been defeated in a baseball game, 12–4, in the play-off for the league championship. It's even more difficult to be glad when your team was favored by 4 runs."

You're right. An attitude of gladness is not your natural attitude in such a situation. It's an attitude that only the Holy Spirit can produce in you. God gives the reason for gladness in James 1:2–4. He says that **testing** produces **endurance** (a toughness of spiritual fiber as we look to God for what He is going to do). With endurance we keep relying on God. We become **perfect** and **complete** when we totally look to Him and away from ourselves. Testing leads to **completeness!** That's why you can be glad after losing 14–4. Your goal is being accomplished. You are becoming more like Jesus.

**There is no such thing as an "athletic set-back" from God's perspective!** Situations often termed "athletic set-backs" are actually **opportunities** to trust God to develop you into a mature person. That is the cause for your gladness.

God allowed the apostle Paul to encounter several situations through which Paul developed a **deep trust in him.** Paul was shipwrecked, imprisoned, stoned, beaten, etc. What was Paul's attitude through each of these difficult situations?

> "And not only this, but we also **exult** in our tribulations; knowing that tribulation brings about perseverance; and perseverance, proven character, and proven character, hope; and hope does not disappoint, because the love of God has been poured out within our hearts through the Holy Spirit who was given to us."
>
> (Romans 5:3–5)

What did Paul do about situations that could be termed "set-backs?" He **exulted** in them. The word "exult" means he actually boasted about his circumstances. He didn't gripe. He wasn't depressed by them. He didn't feel badly about them. That's strange, isn't it? It's natural to be depressed when you're in the midst of a miserable situation.

But remember, the Christian isn't to live a natural life. He is to live a supernatural life through the Holy Spirit. Paul knew each tribulation (difficult situation) did something to build him into the complete man God desired him to be. Paul desired to experience all that God had for him. He wrote that tribulations bring about perseverance. The word "perseverance" implies the bearing up under a burden. It's the same Greek word that James used in James 1:3 for the word "endurance." The pressure was on Paul several times, but he was empowered by the Holy Spirit to **bear** up under the pressure. Pressure was used by God to develop endurance in Paul. But it didn't stop there. He wrote that perseverance (endurance) brings about proven character. The term "proven character" describes someone who has gone through some sort of testing and has been approved. Paul stood the test. His maturity had been approved by God.

Proven character leads to the next stage of development in a Christian. It brings **hope.** The word "hope" refers to the expectation of something in the future. Paul uses it in reference to looking to God for what He is doing **through** the trial or difficult situation. God is not stymied by your situation. In fact, **He either caused it to happen or allowed it to happen for His purpose!** He is in total control.

> "And we know that God causes all things to work together for good to those who love God, to those who are called according to His purpose."
>
> (Romans 8:28)

God's plan for your life is constantly unfolding. The apostle Paul wrote, ". . . for it is God who is at work in you, both to will and to work for His good pleasure" (Philippians 2:13). A situation other people might describe as a "set-back" is actually an **opportunity** for you to see God work according to His plan for your life. Because athletics are a vital part of your life, you can be sure God will work through athletics to conform you into the image of His Son. Paul continued by saying **hope does not disappoint.** That's important to remember. It's easy to be disappointed because of circumstances. But, God is more powerful than any circumstance. Hope does not disappoint because God has a purpose for every difficult situation.

> "We can rejoice, too, when we run into problems and trials for we know that they are good for us—they help us learn to be patient. And patience develops strength of character in us and helps us trust God more each time until finally our hope and faith are strong and steady. Then, when that happens, we will be able to hold our heads high no matter what happens and know that all is well, for we will know how dearly God loves us, and we will feel this warm love everywhere within us because God has given us the Holy Spirit to fill our hearts with His love."
>
> (Romans 3:3–5, The Living Bible)

What we so often see as a defeat, God sees as a steppingstone to victory. For instance, it was natural to see the crucifixion of Jesus Christ as a defeat. His shoulders were dislocated. His back was torn open from the scourge. His face was beaten beyond recognition. Most of His friends had deserted Him. No one spoke up in His defense. Curious bystanders mocked Him as He hung in agony. Even His disciples thought the end had come.

But from God's viewpoint, the **beginning had just begun!** The natural viewpoint saw weakness. God saw power!

The natural viewpoint is our first reaction to a situation if we aren't under the control of the Holy Spirit. With this natural viewpoint, one sees only circumstances. God looks **through** circumstances and sees His **purpose.** Can you imagine our predicament if the crucifixion had not taken place? The penalty for our sins would still be resting on us. The crucifixion also had to take place before the victorious resurrection could happen.

What so often is regarded as a defeat from our natural viewpoint is merely the preparatory stages through which God will demonstrate His power. Gideon, in Judges 7, gives us a graphic example of this. Here are the facts:

1. God called Gideon to lead Israel in battle against the Midianites.

2. Gideon rounded up an army of 33,000 men to do battle against an army of 135,000.

3. God told Gideon that he had **too many** men. "And the Lord said to Gideon, 'The people who are with you are too many for Me to give Midian into their hands, lest Israel become boastful saying, "My own power has delivered me" ' "(Judges 7:2).

4. Gideon's army was finally cut back to **only 300 men!**

5. The result? God, through 300 men, defeated an army of 135,000 trained soldiers!

6. Why only 300 men? God received all the glory! It was through His power that certain defeat was turned into victory.

God demonstrates His power through human weakness. The apostle Paul was bothered by a physical ailment. Although he asked God three times to remove it, God DID NOT remove Paul's ailment. Through this experience Paul wrote about God's perspective.

> "And He has said to me, 'My grace is sufficient for you, for power is **perfected** in weakness.' Most gladly, therefore, will I rather boast about my weaknesses, that the **power of Christ** may **dwell** in me. Therefore I am well content with weaknesses, with insults, with distresses, with persecutions, with difficulties, for Christ's sake; for when I am weak, **then I am strong.**"
>
> (2 Corinthians 12:9–10)

A conscious alertness to the following biblical facts will give you God's perspective on every difficult situation that could be considered an "athletic setback."

1. God's goal for you is that you become conformed to the very likeness of Jesus Christ.

> "For whom He foreknew, He also predestined to become conformed to the image of His Son, that He might be the first-born among many brethren."
>
> (Romans 8:29)

2. God will cause **everything** (including situations that could be termed "athletic set-backs") to work together to build you toward the purpose He has for your life.

"And we know that God **causes all things** to work together for good to those who love God, to those who are called according to His purpose.

(Romans 8:28)

3. God desires you to thank Him for every situation. You can sincerely do this, knowing that every trial can be used by God to bring you closer toward your true goal—being conformed to the image of Jesus Christ.

". . . In everything give thanks; for this is God's will for you in Christ Jesus."

(1 Thessalonians 5:18)

You can thank Him because He is giving you endurance. He is toughening your spiritual fiber as you look to Him for what He is doing. You can thank Him because He is making you perfect and complete.

From the world's viewpoint, your situation is an "athletic set-back." From God's viewpoint, it's an opportunity to see Him use the situation in accomplishing His desired will. The experience of a friend is a good example of this. At the National Collegiate Weightlifting Championships my friend had a good chance to set a new record in one of the lifts. However, when he attempted his lifts, he was unable to succeed with even his starting poundages. As a result, he failed to place in the contest.

My friend looked at his failure from God's perspective. He didn't understand why he was unable to succeed with a poundage he had previously lifted with ease. Yet, he felt confident that God either caused or allowed his failure for a purpose. That night, when he phoned long distance to his parents, they thought he finished first because of the enthusiasm still in his voice. Some time later, his father asked how he was able to be so content after failing to place in the most important contest of his life. My friend then shared with his father how Jesus had given him a perspective of trusting God for the results. God used this athlete's attitude toward failure to help his father see the reality of Jesus Christ living in his life. Soon after that, his father believed in Jesus and accepted Him into his life. God accomplished one of His purposes—bringing my friend's father to Himself—through a "failure" in a weighlifting contest.

**There is no such thing as an athletic set-back for the Christian athlete!** Every trial that comes your way has been allowed by God for a reason. He is concerned about you reaching your true goal for living—to be conformed to the likeness of Jesus Christ. He will work **everything** toward that end result. He also may have additional reasons for causing and allowing situations to happen, one of which is bringing a person to Himself. By trusting in God, there are **no defeats.** In Him, there are **no set-backs.** There are only **opportunities** to see Him at work and make you more complete in Jesus Christ.

## FOR DISCUSSION

1. Describe some of your athletic set-backs and what affect they have had on you.

2. Discuss the meaning and implications of the following verses and how they apply to your athletic performance.

   John 16:23
   James 1:2–4
   Romans 5:3–5
   Romans 8:28

2 Corinthians 12:9–10
1 Thessalonians 5:18

3. Why is there no such thing as an athletic set-back to a Christian athlete?

4. In regard to athletic "set-backs," discuss the fact God either caused it to happen or allowed it to happen for His purpose.

5. Describe how, in your own athletic experience, God has turned defeat into victory.

## CHAPTER 17

# THE DOULOS ATHLETE

A strange sight occurred on the pitcher's mound in a baseball game between the Dodgers and Cardinals in the early 1940's. Fred Fitzsimmons was pitching for the Dodgers with two outs and a two run lead in the ninth inning. The Cardinals had the bases loaded with Johnny Mize, their best hitter, coming up next. Fitzsimmons, though in somewhat of a difficult situation, was eager to face Mize. Dodger manager Leo Durocher decided to make a pitching change. He called time-out and went to the pitcher's mound the same as he had done in so many games before. Only this time he was facing a defiant Fred Fitzsimmons.

Fitzsimmons refused to be taken out. Durocher insisted. Fitzsimmons refused. What a sight the fans had as they couldn't believe their eyes. The two men argued with each other for about five minutes before Durocher finally gave up and went back to the dugout.

Now all Fitzsimmons had to do was face the Cardinals best hitter with the bases loaded. It must have seemed easy after triumphantly defying Leo Durocher. After moving the count to three balls and two strikes, Fitzsimmons finally struck out Johnny Mize. Even Durocher could live with that ending!

Most people left the ball park thinking it might pay, after all, to defy a leader's instructions. You have many opportunities in your athletic career to challenge your coach's orders. Most likely you won't challenge them quite as drastically as Fred Fitzsimmons did. A challenge can be an unspoken attitude as well as an outward action.

Do you have a responsibility to obey your coach in everything, or as a Christian athlete, are there occasions when you do not have to obey him? What is your responsibility when you don't agree with your coach's approach to training or his game plan? What do you do when you don't agree with his use of substitutes or his manner of administering discipline? What is your responsibility if your coach directs the team as a dictator?

A couple of years ago I had asked a weightlifting coach to train me for the upcoming weightlifting state championships. Although I had trained myself for many years, I knew this man would be able to help improve my weightlifting technique. He had certain ideas on how an athlete should train to get top results.

The evening came for my first workout with him. After warming up by stretching, I asked my coach what he wanted me to do. He told me to begin power snatching. After doing several of them, my shoulders began to hurt due to the wide hand spacing used in this lift. I told him about the pain and that I thought I should practice a different lift—one that would put less stress on my shoulders.

I'll never forget the unsympathetic look he gave me. He knew there was no injury to my shoulders. It was just the pain of lifting weights to an overhead position with tired arms and shoulders. His reply to my request was straight to the point. He said, "I told you to practice the power snatch. That's what I want you to do. Now get with it."

My first reaction was to tell him a few things he should learn about coaching and stomp off to the locker room. But I did not give in to my natural tendency because the Holy Spirit immediately brought two very important biblical concepts to my mind. First of all, I remembered my role in the chain-of-command. Secondly, I remembered the attitude God wants me to have as I carry out my role assignment.

## THE CHAIN-OF-COMMAND

God has placed the athlete in a chain-of-command. The chain-of-command is a line of authority. It always has at least one leader and one follower. For example, the head coach of a football team is the leader and each player is a follower. A chain-of-command can also have more than one leader. A football team has a head coach and several assistant coaches. Each assistant coach is also a follower in relationship to the head coach. The line of authority, then, of a football team would be head coach, assistant coaches, team captain and the rest of the players.

The chain-of-command is a biblical concept designed by God to help us function at our maximum effectiveness—where there is a minimum of confusion. Each person in the chain has a clear cut responsibility. If no one knew his responsibility in relation to other people, there would be total confusion. For instance, can you imagine what would happen at a busy intersection if no one paid attention to traffic signals? (There is even a chain-of-command in traffic regulators.) There would be several collisions a day.

When the light is red, each motorist has a responsibility to stop. When it is green, they have the responsibility to go. Traffic signals have been placed at the proper corners by people who want to have motorists get safely through the intersection. For a similar reason, God has given us the chain-of-command to help each person know his responsibility and function at the highest level of efficiency. Confusion reigns when people do not carry out the role assigned to them by the chain-of-command. Biblical texts to illustrate the chain-of-command are: Genesis 3:16; I Corinthians 11:3; Romans 13:1–2; Ephesians 5:23; 6:1; 6:5–9; Colossians 3:18–20; 3:22; Titus 3:1 and I Peter 2:13–15.

When my coach told me to continue practicing the lift that caused my shoulders to ache, I realized that my role in the chain-of-command was to obey his leading. It didn't matter if I agreed with his approach or not. As long as he was my coach, his responsibility was to give me instructions and my responsibility was to follow them.

The same is true in your responsibility to your coach. You might not agree with him on every point, but your role is to carry out his assignments. The attitude you have as you carry out each assignment will determine if you are a winner in God's sight.

## THE DOULOS ROLE

When I went back to the lifting platform to practice the same lift, I could have simply gone through the motions. The purpose of the practice session would have been wasted for the most part. However, I returned to practice the lift with a new sense of enthusiasm because I had the willing attitude of doing it my coach's way. An athlete who has a willing attitude to do it his coach's way could be described as a DOULOS athlete.

You might not be acquainted with this word "doulos" (due-loss). The apostle Paul used it frequently to describe his relationship with Jesus. "Doulos" is the Greek word for bond-servant. Paul wrote in Romans 1:1, "Paul, a **bond-servant** of Christ Jesus, called as an apostle, set apart for the gospel of God . . ." The word "doulos" is actually taken from another Greek word "deo" which means "to bind." The person who is a doulos is completely BOUND to another person. His will is completely swallowed up in the will of the other person.

An athlete's natural response to a command he doesn't agree with is stubborness.

He might go through the motions of carrying out the command from his coach, but his heart just isn't in it.

However, **a doulos athlete's** will is bound to the command of his coach. For instance, if his coach yells "Jump!" the doulos athlete doesn't waste time asking "why." He puts everything he has into the jump **Immediately!**

The word "doulos" can be contrasted with "therapon," which is another Greek word for servant. The therapon has a choice in whether or not he wants to carry out the command. If he doesn't like it, he can always quit. **The doulos has no choice!** He is completely at the disposal of the person for whom he is a doulos. Any desire on his leader's part results in **instant action** by the doulos. This is the word Paul used to describe his responsiveness to God. Any desire on God's part became instant action on Paul's part.

The reason my weightlifting workout went so successfully when I returned to the platform to lift was because I looked upon myself as **a doulos** to my coach. I wanted my actions to be the instant and complete response to my coach's desire for me. I knew that by being obedient to my coach, I was also being obedient to God.

> "Servants, be submissive to your masters with all respect . . . for this finds favor with God."
>
> (I Peter 2:18–20)

A chain-of-command operates at 100% efficiency only when each person in a "followership" role looks upon himself as a **doulos** or bondservant to his leader. As an athlete, you are in a "followership" role to your coach. He is the leader; you are the follower. As a **doulos athlete,** your will is completely swallowed up in the will of your coach.

## JESUS—THE PERFECT DOULOS

Jesus demonstrated TOTAL SUBMISSIVENESS throughout His entire life. It was most notable for us in the Garden of Gethsemane shortly before He was taken captive. Jesus left three of His disciples and went **a** little further into the garden. He fell on the ground in agony. He prayed, "All things are possible for Thee; remove this cup from Me; yet not what I will, but **what Thou wilt"** (Mark 14:36).

Jesus had a desire to go through with His Father's plan, but in a different way. He didn't want to experience the torturous crucifixion or the painful separation from His Father. But He had the attitude of a **doulos** when He said, "Yet not what I will, but what Thou wilt." A short time later Jesus subjected

Himself to the crucifixion. His Father's desire was His action.

It's interesting to note here that a **doulos** athlete has the right to go to his coach and express his feelings. Jesus expressed His feelings and desire to His Father in the Garden of Gethsemane. His **doulos** attitude was that He would wholeheartedly do what He was told to do. A **doulos** athlete has the privilege of expressing his desires as long as it is accompanied by the willingness to do whatever he's told.

God's perspective on winning refers to your mental and physical intensity directed toward an action. But it also refers to what attitude you have toward your coach. As a winner, you totally release yourself toward performing like Jesus in every situation throughout your athletic performance. That means you are to have the SAME attitude toward your coach that Jesus had toward His Father—total submissiveness.

Jesus was the perfect doulos. He was in instant and complete obedience to His Father. His greatest desire was to accomplish His Father's purpose. He released His entire self toward doing that even when it meant He would experience a painful death.

The **doulos athlete,** then, is one who **instantly** obeys every command of his coach. He puts his entire self into it. This is one way you can represent Jesus in your athletic performance.

## YOUR RESPONSIBILITY

The following questions concerning your relationship with your coach will help you understand the implications of being a **doulos athlete.**

1. Is your coach responsible for letting you know the details of his motives, strategy or any other area that affects you as an athlete?

Your coach is responsible to his leader for your care on the practice field and in competition. This is an awesome responsibility. He is **not responsible,** however, to relate to you all that is on his mind. He can do so if he should choose to communicate with his team this way, but he does not have the responsibility to do so. He would have that responsibility only if his leader commanded it. You might have some consolation in that even Jesus did not know every detail of His Father's plan so far as the timing. Jesus' disciples questioned Him concerning the exact time when the last things on earth would take place. Jesus answered, "But of that day or hour no one knows, not even the angels in heaven, nor the Son, but the Father alone" (Mark 13:32).

2. What if your coach is not a good doulos to the authorities ahead of him in the chain-of-command? Does that release you from your doulos role?

No, it doesn't. Peter wrote in I Peter 2:18–20, "Servants, be submissive to your masters with **all respect,** not only to those who are good and gentle, but also to those who are **unreasonable.** For this finds favor, if for the sake of conscience toward God **a** man bears up under sorrows when suffering unjustly. For what credit is there if, when you sin and are harshly treated, you endure it with patience? But if, when you do what is right and suffer for it you **patiently endure it,** this finds **favor** with God."

3. If you think you know more than your coach in a particular area, is it all right to do what you think is

best, rather than do what he says if there is a conflict between the two?

One thing to keep in mind is any time God should choose to do so, He could change the thinking of your coach. God did so with Pharaoh when it served His best interest (Exodus 8–12).

If God does not choose to change your coach's thinking, He wants to **build in your** life. Your responsibility is to carry out your coach's commands and desires no matter how more knowledgeable you are. Remember, you can go to him in private and express your wishes, but only with the sincere attitude of doing what He decides.

4. Does God want you to be a **doulos athlete** even when your coach makes mistakes in judgment and personal communications?

Your coach is responsible to the authority above him. If that authority should decide he makes too many mistakes, he could be replaced. You still have the responsibility of being a **doulos athlete** even when your coach makes bad judgments or communicates poorly.

5. What should you do if you think your coach is doing a poor job but the authority above won't re place him?

This is a concern for the authority above him. It should not weigh on your mind. When we take on responsibilities and concerns that God has not given us in the chain-of-command, our mind becomes encumbered with unnecessary weight. Your effectiveness as an athlete will increase as you learn to LET GO of those concerns that do not fall within your realm of responsibility.

6. As a **doulos athlete,** what should be your response if your coach gives you a command that violates God's Word in the Bible?

God has instituted the chain-of-command within which you operate as an athlete. Unfortunately, each chain-of-command potentially has leaders who do not listen to God for their instructions. Once in a while they will give a command without really being aware that it violates God's Word. If this is your situation, go to your coach and share with him your concern about how his instructions affect you as a Christian. Be sure to do this in an understanding manner so as not to accuse him of being against God. For instance, you might say, "Coach, a couple of years ago I wouldn't have had any problem going along with that, but since I've come to rely on Jesus Christ, I've got a real problem with it. Could we talk about it?"

Remember, most likely your coach didn't give you the instructions to oppose God. However, he did have a reason. Try to discern what that reason was. You can even offer him another course of action that would accomplish what he wanted with his instructions. This is what the prophet Daniel did. Daniel was in captivity. The king ordered him and other young men to eat certain rich foods. Daniel knew the food was not God's choice for him so he offered another course of action. He discerned that the king's command was given for all the young men to eat the rich food to make them strong and healthy. Daniel requested permission to eat his own chosen food for ten days. If, after ten days, he was not stronger and healthier than the other young men, then he would eat whatever he was ordered to eat. He was allowed to eat his food for the ten days. After ten days Daniel was found to be stronger and healthier than the other men. From that time onward he was exempt from eating the king's food and was allowed to eat according to his convictions (Daniel 1:8–16).

Let's use an extreme situation. Let's say your coach gives you an order to deliberately rough up a player on the other team. After you let your coach know that, as a Christian, you have a problem with carrying out his instructions, you suggest a possible alternate course of action to accomplish his purpose. For the sake of illustration, let's assume that his reason for such instructions was to quickly remove from the game an opposing athlete who was being very effective against his team. You offer your coach a possible strategy of nullifying this athlete's effectiveness while keeping within the rules. If your coach accepts your proposal or decides against his original instructions, your approaching him was well worth it. On the other hand, let's say your coach still insists on you carrying out his original instructions that definitely violate God's way of doing it. You're in a difficult situation, aren't you? If you tell your coach you can't follow his orders, he could bench you and possibly cut you from the team. Your future career in athletics could then be jeopardized.

If you go back into the game with no intention of carrying out his orders, you are in disobedience to God's chain-of-command.

In Acts 4:18 Peter and John were ordered not to talk to anybody about Jesus. This was in clear violation of God's command in Matthew 28:18–20, where Jesus gave His followers the Great Commission to teach about Him **everywhere.** Peter and John responded, "Whether it is right in the sight of God to give heed to you rather than to God, you be the judge; for we cannot stop speaking what we have seen and heard" (Acts 4:19–20).

If you do as your coach orders, you will not be representing Jesus Christ. What do you do? You have a responsibility to obey God's Word. You can say something like, "I'm sorry, coach. I want to give you everything I have, but I can't carry out your order." Remember, God is in complete charge of the situation. If he has a future career in athletics for you, nothing can stop it, even if you were cut from the team. Keep in mind:

**1. God is intensely interested in you.**

> "But the very hairs of your head are all numbered."
>
> (Matthew 10:30)

**2. God has given you abilities for a purpose.**

> "The Lord has made everything for its (His) own purpose . . ."
>
> (Proverbs 16:4)

**3. God works every circumstance toward His purpose.**

> "And we know that all that happens to us is working for our good if we love God and are fitting into His plans."
>
> (Romans 8:28, The Living Bible)

You're willing to become a champion for Jesus Christ. The real test is, are you willing to be cut from the team for Him? Appendix V gives you many of God's Words concerning various matters in your athletics. Be sure your ideas, as you talk to your coach, are accurately based on God's Word. Most of the time your coach is not even aware he is giving instructions that violate God's Word. Be discerning and in the Holy Spirit's control when you approach him. Don't accuse, but inform him of your feelings.

## REPROGRAMMING YOUR MIND

Jesus was the perfect DOULOS. The following two methods can help reprogram your mind so you will respond to your coach as Jesus would respond.

1. In preparation for each training session and actual competition, picture you handing yourself over to your coach. You can be creative in your imagination. You might see yourself standing on a big palm of a hand, being presented to your coach. Perhaps you might see yourself with a shackle on your leg attached to one on your coach's leg. The main thing you want to accomplish, whichever way you picture yourself being handed over to your coach, is to see yourself as a complete **doulos athlete.** He is your leader. Your desire is to carry out your coach's instructions, and thus accomplish God's purpose. Always remember, God can change your coach's instructions any time He desires to do so. Your allegiance to your coach can help strengthen your allegiance to God. Each takes a denial of self.

2. Picture your actions as a complete **oneness** with your coach's instructions. You might see yourself putting a total concentrated effort into running specific patterns your coach tells you to run. If he says "Jump!" you're already two feet off the ground.

The idea in these two exercises of the mind is to see your coach as God sees him. Your coach is the head of you in your athletic chain-of-command. These two exercises will help you see him this way. Then you will more easily respond to your coach's instructions with a positive enthusiasm.

My weightlifting workout was excellent because I understood my role in the athletic chain-of-command and I viewed myself as a **doulos athlete.** I didn't even notice the discomfort to my shoulders when I had the **doulos** attitude.

Your coach can try all the possible motivational techniques and be a failure as a leader if you don't commit yourself to being a **doulos** athlete. Your "followership" will free him to develop his leadership abilities. A person is not an effective leader unless someone is following. You can contribute greatly to your coach's leadership by developing your attitude as a **doulos athlete!**

## FOR DISCUSSION

1. What is the chain-of-command and why has God given it to us?
2. Describe the different chains-of-command within which you function.
3. What is a doulos athlete and how does that role apply to your athletic performance?
4. Contrast the "therapon" and "doulos" athlete and discuss the affect they would have on a team.
5. In what way do you, as a doulos athlete, have a right to go to your coach to question an assignment (Mark 14:36)?
6. Discuss each of the six questions concerning obedience to your coach and the implications they have for you as a doulos athlete.

7. What is the procedure you are to follow if your coach asks you to carry out an assignment that violates God's Word?

8. In what ways can you, as a doulos athlete, contribute to your coach's leadership?

# CHAPTER 18

# THE PERFECT TEAM SPIRIT

No athletic team can perform at a greater capacity than the individual abilities comprising it. Yet, if those abilities don't blend together in just the right **climate,** or **spirit,** their full potential will **not** be achieved in a team effort. Players on a west coast football team discovered the truth of this statement as their play improved after beginning to work together as a team. One of the players said, "We had an awful lot of guys who were strictly out for themselves, and our team was almost nothing but a bunch of ego trips." This team lost games they should have won if only their talent was to be considered. They not only lost the games, but their tempers as well. They clashed with each other as well as with their coaches. What changed them from being a defeated team one year to an undefeated team and the national champions the next year? They had most of the same players. One thing was different. They now had a unity. Several players were either already Christians or recently had become Christians. They began to meet together in discussion and prayer. Soon they were pulling for each other and encouraging each other. It was contagious. Even the players who did not believe in Christ appreciated the positive affect the group of Christians had on the team.

## ONE PLAYER CAN BE A NEGATIVE INFLUENCE

The Bible has many principles that can be applied to developing maximum team spirit. The usual kind of team spirit is the "RAH RAH" and "GO GO" type.

This is good and certainly part of it, but there can be so much more. Before we get into how team spirit develops, let's look at the influence just one person with a bad attitude can have on your team.

Such an athlete can affect the rest of the athletes in any one of the following three ways:

1. He can influence other athletes to **share** his poor attitude.

2. He can cause the other athletes to at least passively pay attention to him, even though they don't share his attitude.

3. He can cause the other athletes to try to help him overcome his poor attitude.

The first two reactions of athletes will lessen the effectiveness of the team. For instance, if you began to **share** his poor attitude, you would help to produce a stifling effect on your own performance. Proverbs 23:7 reminds us, "For as he thinks within himself, so he is . . ." Your negative thoughts will reproduce themselves in negative actions. If you do not share his poor attitude, but are passively **distracted** by him, you cannot focus your full attention on the task at hand. Your mind cannot focus with 100% of its efficiency on more than one thing at a time. The third reaction is part of what's involved in developing team spirit.

## COMMON TEAM SPIRIT DEPENDS ON CIRCUMSTANCES

Team spirit is the missing ingredient on a team where athletes are not totally united toward a common purpose. The team possessing team spirit seems to have an extra spark. It has a climate where the athletes are truly interested in each other and moving toward their task **together.**

Unfortunately, on most teams, the usual type of team spirit comes and goes, depending on the **circumstances.** If a particular task is equally important to each athlete (e.g., defeating the cross-town rival), a bond of togetherness forms that draws out the best from each athlete. You are able to see a mutual encouraging of each other.

Boxers on the United States 1972 Olympic Team tasted a bit of team spirit, but it was based upon circumstances. One of the boxers received what his teammates referred to as a "poor decision." This inspired them to make up for that defeat. Each boxer fought with new determination until the affect of the circumstances wore off.

## THE HIGHEST FORM OF TEAM SPIRIT

As a Christian athlete, you have an opportunity to be instrumental in developing the highest form of team spirit on your team. It is a team spirit that does not waver with new circumstances. It is as real in the midst of a "losing" season as it is in a drive for the conference title. The nature of this team spirit is explained by the following three facts:

1. Team spirit empowered by human emotions will be inconsistent. Only that empowered by God will be consistent.

> "Every good thing bestowed [e.g., team spirit] and every perfect gift is from above, coming down from the Father of lights, with whom **there is no variation,** or shifting shadow."
>
> (James 1:17)

2. Actions are a better teacher than words alone in communicating team spirit to other teammates.

> "Even so faith, if it has no works [action], **is dead,** being by itself."
>
> (James 2:17)

3. Team spirit must **begin with you.** The apostle Paul knew that the reality of Christian living must be seen in him so others could have an example to follow.

> "I exhort you therefore, be imitators of me [Paul]."
>
> (1 Corinthians 4:16)

God's type of team spirit has each of these qualities. It is empowered by God, through the Holy Spirit, prompting you to take a specific course of action so that it can be demonstrated to your teammates.

## YOUR RESPONSIBILITY

From a biblical perspective, here are three things you can do to enable your team to experience the **highest form of team spirit.**

1. **Be prepared** to initiate action that demonstrates this kind of team spirit. You prepare by being sure you are controlled by the Holy Spirit. The apostle Paul wrote in Ephesians 5:18, ". . . be filled [controlled] with the Spirit . . ." Any action you take outside the control of the Holy Spirit is superficial. The Holy Spirit is the source of this highest form of team spirit.

**2. Use words.** This highest form of team spirit is vocal. In this way it is similar to the standard type of emotional team spirit. Both use words. But here the similarity ends. The words you will use are more than the "Go get 'em!" remarks so easily given. The apostle Paul explains what kind of words you are to use:

> "Let no unwholesome word proceed from your mouth, but only such a word as is good for **edification** according to the **need of the moment,** that it may give grace to those who hear."
>
> (Ephesians 4:29)

The word "unwholesome" refers to something rotten and putrid. If dead fish happen to be in the sun for three or four days, the odor could be described as "unwholesome." Paul uses it in this passage to describe any words coming from a Christian that are not representative of Jesus Christ. They don't reflect His thoughts.

Paul would not use the word "unwholesome" to describe the words of a Christian who is fully controlled by the Holy Spirit. He's realistic. His writings indicate a full awareness on his part that the Christian life is a constant struggle between the spiritual and carnal. Athletics have a tendency to draw out the natural reactions of a Christian faster than they do his spiritual response.

The point of what Paul wrote is if you happen to be away from the Holy Spirit's control you should **resist** allowing words to come out of your mouth that very well might reflect your natural attitudes.

Let's say one of your teammates has done something to upset you. You're angry. You have just the "perfect" thing to say that will really "chop" him down. Stop! God wants you to keep from saying it. Instead of satisfying your desire for the moment, consciously commit yourself to the Holy Spirit's control (chapter 4).

What quality of words does God command you to say at that moment of temptation? ". . . only such a word as is good for **edification** according to the need of the moment . . ." The word "edification" refers to the building of a house. Paul uses that descriptive word in reference to an often **slow** and **deliberate** process. It takes time to build into a person's life with words.

On the athletic scene, this is often a forgotten art. Where every man is usually looking out for his own worth, it is not natural to tell a teammate something that will build him into a better person. Let's say you notice a baseball player looking very dejected as he walks back to the dugout. He just struck out for the third time in a row. He doesn't need anyone to tell him he's having a bad day at bat. He knew that before he swung and missed for the third strike. What he needs is someone to understand him.

He needs to know you accept him regardless of how well he does at bat.

3. **Take action.** Team spirit will not evolve of itself. We have a guideline from Paul concerning what sort of action you're to take:

> "Therefore **encourage one another,** and **build up one another,** just as you also are doing."
>
> (1 Thessalonians 5:11)

The context of this passage is directed toward the encouragement and building up of other Christians. It explains what action you are to take regarding your Christian teammates. The word "encourage" means to call someone to your side, usually with the intention of **helping him** in some respect. It doesn't refer to idle chatter. It carries with it the effect of encouraging the person with **words** and **actions** that meet his particular needs. For instance, let's say that one of your football teammates doesn't know how to use an effective stiff-arm. As a result, he frequently gets tackled and stopped short of the yards he should be gaining.

He needs some instruction. Some of your teammates might even be down on him for frequently getting tackled so easily. You take the positive approach of 1 Thessalonians 5:11. On the sideline, you show him how to employ the stiff-arm effectively. You might introduce your desire to help by saying something like, "You've got some good running ability. I think there's one move I can show you that possibly could make you even more effective." In doing this, you're helping him where he has a particular need.

With this new knowledge of how to avoid getting tackled as easily, the runner is able to utilize more of his athletic potential.

The word "build" in 1 Thessalonians 5:11 would describe the **building** of a house. You first begin with a solid foundation. It's the most important part of a house's construction and it takes time to build. Once the foundation is ready, frames are built. This also takes time. People passing by a construction site are often disappointed that progress doesn't seem to be taking place when the men are working on the foundation and frames. Then, seemingly out of nowhere, the frames are up and there is a resemblance of a house. That's the connotation of 1 Thessalonians 5:11. Just as the building of a house's foundation and frames takes time, so does the building of your teammates. It takes time to lay a solid foundation upon which to build maturity. You might make every effort to help one of your teammates, but he just doesn't seem to respond. He doesn't seem to appreciate your help. Your natural reaction is to forget him and let him help himself. But, according to 1 Thessalonians 5:11, God desires you to continue laying the solid foundation in that individual's life.

What a tremendous witness this is to non-Christians on your team. When they see **love in action,** they see the reality of Jesus Christ in your life.

Jesus told His men, "A new commandment I give to you, that you love one another, even as I have loved you, that you also love one another. By this **all men** will know that you are My disciples, if you have love for one another" (John 3:34–35). God desires you to actively and openly give of yourself to others in His family to help develop them more into the likeness of Jesus Christ.

God's highest form of team spirit is a climate developed through His means and empowered by His Spirit. He works through Christians to convey His quality of spirit to an entire team. It begins with you as the Holy Spirit works through your life. It generates from you as you are totally available and receptive to carry out God's commands.

It takes time, but it's worth it! You not only will see the highest quality of spirit become a reality on your team, but you will see more readiness on the part of your teammates to learn about Jesus. They will see His quality of life in you.

## FOR DISCUSSION

1. Discuss two factors that determine your team's level of performance and how they relate to team spirit.

2. How does a poor attitude affect team spirit?

3. Why is it important to have team spirit?

4. Discuss three Scriptural principles that develop the highest form of team spirit and how they relate to your athletic performance.

5. Discuss the three actions you can take to help your team experience the highest form of team spirit. Be specific in your application.

## TALK OUTLINE

I. Your Team's Level of Performance.
   A. Two factors determine your team's level of performance.
      1. The athletic abilities of each individual.
      2. The blending together of each individual's athletic abilities with those of his teammates.
   B. The effect poor attitudes have on a team.
      1. Cause other athletes to share his poor attitude.
      2. Cause other athletes to passively pay attention to him though they don't share his poor attitude.
      3. Cause other athletes to try to help him overcome his poor attitude.

II. Team Spirit Draws Out the Best in an Athlete.
   A. Most team spirit is determined by circumstances.
   B. A team cannot experience the highest form of team spirit without its members encouraging one another.

III. Three Scriptural Principles to Develop the Highest Form of Team Spirit.
   A. The only constant team spirit is that empowered by God. Human emotions cause it to vary (James 1:17).

B. Actions or examples are a better teacher than words alone in communicating team spirit (James 2:17).
C. Team spirit *begins in you* for others to see (1 Corinthians 4:16).

IV. Three Actions For You to Take to Experience the Highest Form of Team Spirit.
A. Preparation (Ephesians 5:18).
B. Words (Ephesians 4:29).
1. "Unwholesome" refers to something rotten and putrid.
2. Paul would not use the word "unwholesome" to describe the words of a Christian who is fully controlled by the Holy Spirit.
3. "Edification" is a building up with words.
4. Be sensitive to your teammates' needs and verbally build in their lives.
C. Action (1 Thessalonians 5:11).
1. "Encourage" means to call someone to your side, usually with the intention of helping him in some respect. It carries with it the effect of words and actions that meet his needs.
2. "Build" is used to describe the building of a house; that is, it takes time.
3. Openly give of yourself to your Christian teammates to help develop them into more of a likeness of Jesus. This is love in action (John 13:34–35).

V. God's Highest Form of Team Spirit is a Climate Developed Through His Means and Empowered by His Spirit.
A. It all begins with available Christians—you!
B. It takes time, but the results are worth it.

## APPENDIX I

# THE QUIET TIME

### by Dan'l Hollis

The quiet time is that part of the day when we spend time alone with God. It is a time basically made up of Bible study and prayer. The purpose of the quiet time is to develop a love relationship with God.

We see the importance of having a quiet time from the conversation Jesus had as He visited some close friends (Luke 10:38–42). As Jesus entered Bethany, Martha welcomed Him into her home. Mary, Martha's sister, sat at Jesus' feet listening to His every word, while Martha was busily cleaning and preparing dinner for her guests. Finally, Martha could take it no longer. She was doing all the hard, tedious housework while Mary was just sitting at Jesus' feet. Martha asked Jesus, "Lord, do You not care that my sister left me to do all the serving alone? Tell her to help me." Did Jesus jump up and say, "Wow! I'm really sorry, let's all get busy. We've spent too much time at this." No, not at all! What Jesus said was, "Mary has chosen the good part." "Good" means worthy of admiration. It's good in relation to something else. He was telling Martha that Mary was doing something more admirable than she was doing. Jesus was not condemning her working. He was simply saying spending time at His feet (quiet time) is better than being busy—even if it's for the Lord. Notice He also said, "You're worried and bothered about too many things; there's only one thing necessary." Time with God!

Jesus put a great prize on others spending time at His feet and learning of His Father. This is what He desires us to do.

We, like Martha, say, "Lord, I haven't got time." And Christ replies, "Then you're **really** too busy." The most important thing in life is time with the Lord. If your schedule is too full, then you might have to cut something out. If you can't eliminate anything, then you might have to get up earlier or go to bed later. Spending time with God is the most important thing you can do—so important that it shouldn't be neglected. Notice Jesus also said, ". . . the good part, which shall not be taken away from her." What Mary learned will last for eternity. She was growing in the knowledge of Jesus Christ.

Now Jesus practiced what He preached. Let's look at His life and learn from His example.

> "But the news about Him was spreading even farther, and great multitudes were gathering to hear Him and to be healed of their sickness. But He Himself would often slip away to the wilderness and pray."
>
> (Luke 5:15–16)

> "And He came out and proceeded as was His custom to the Mount of Olives; . . . and He knelt down to pray."
>
> (Luke 22:39, 40)

The Bible tells us of the frequency of Jesus' quiet times. It says, "He would often slip away," and "As was His custom." Jesus, as a pattern of life, spent time alone with His Father. Notice it was His custom and He did it in a certain place. If Christ, the Godman, needed to spend time—a lot of time—alone with His Father, then how much more time do we need to spend!

We are told in Luke 5:15 that He had been preaching and healing people. Surprisingly, in the midst of a good, busy activity, He slipped away to spend time alone with His Father. He knew the importance of a quiet time and didn't neglect it. He made time. Maybe that's what you'll have to do. *Make time.*

## PRACTICAL APPLICATION

1. Choose a regular time and place that's best suited for you. What is right for me is possibly not right for you. Your time and place might even change from day to day. Choose a time when your mind is most alert. That will be up to you. I know of a person who has his quite time from 2:00 A.M. to 4:00 A.M. That's good for him but I'd fall asleep. So pick a time that suits you.

2. Spend time reading the Bible and praying. These topics are covered in Appendices II and III.

3. The length of time depends upon you. This probably will increase as it becomes more a part of your life style. You might want to spend five to ten minutes in the morning each day reading a chapter of the Bible, then praying about your activities for the day.

Stick to it like a workout. Sometimes you don't feel like working out, but you do so because you want to improve. The same is true for a quiet time. This is where you improve spiritually. Satan's greatest desire is to see that you don't improve spiritually. Therefore, he will do whatever he can to keep you from spending time with God. He will try to distract you from your quiet time even with good things, such as sleep, fun times, fellowship with other Christians, etc.

Your quiet time could be compared to developing a friendship with someone. By spending time talking, listening, and enjoying one another, you'll develop a deep love relationship. The same is true spiritually. As you spend time with God, you will develop that love relationship. God desires our daily time in fellowship, that our love for Him may grow.

The main purpose of the quiet time is not what we can get out of it, but surprisingly what we can give to God. We do benefit from it, of course, but our attitude needs to be one of **giving** to God—our praise, worship and our entire self.

God actually seeks our praise and worship which brings Him joy and pleasure. Knowing that developing our love relationship actually brings God delight, how can our quiet time ever be the same?

May we, as Mary did, "choose the best thing"**—time with Him!**

## APPENDIX II

# HOW TO STUDY THE BIBLE

### by Dan'l Hollis

Our fellowship with God is a two way communication. It involves 1) **prayer**—where we share our heart with God and, 2) **Bible study**—where God shares His heart with us. God has graciously given the Bible to study. It's important for two reasons. First, it enables us to know what God is saying and doing in the world today. Secondly, it enables us to have a closer fellowship with God. Becoming a student of God's Word (the Bible) and deepening our fellowship go hand in hand.

God has given us the Holy Spirit to open our eyes to see the truths of God's Word as we study it. The Bible states that the Holy Spirit is given to teach us all things and to continue to bring to our remembrance all Christ has taught (1 John 2:27 and John 14:26).

The apostle Paul explains that the Holy Spirit uses God's Word to teach us the depths of God.

> "But just as it is written, 'Things which eye has not seen and ear has not heard, and which have not entered the heart of man, all that God has prepared for those who love Him.' For to us God revealed them through the Spirit; for the Spirit searches all things, even the depths of God."
>
> (1 Corinthians 2:9–10).

## THE BIBLE IS SPIRITUAL FOOD (JEREMIAH 15:16, PSALMS 119:103)

We will become physically sick if we don't eat food and eventually starvation will result. The same is true spiritually. We will become spiritually sick if we don't eat spiritual food (God's Word).

## THE BIBLE WAS WRITTEN TO CHANGE LIVES

The apostle Paul tells us in a letter to Timothy that God's Word is adequate to change our lives.

> "All Scripture is inspired by God and profitable for *teaching,* for *reproof,* for *correction,* for *instruction in righteousness;* that the man of God may be adequate, equipped for every good work."
>
> (2 Timothy 3:16–17).

He literally was saying that EVERY Scripture inspired by God is profitable. This means the whole Bible is profitable for us.

The Bible is designed by God to do the following according to 2 Timothy 3:16–17:

1) Instruct us (teaching)

2) Expose the thoughts and intents of our heart and show us what we're really like (reproof)

3) Correct and restore us to a close fellowship with God (correction and instruction)

To gain all that God has for us in the Bible, it must be studied in detail as well as read. A whole new experience of living is yours as you study God's Word.

## HELPFUL HINTS ON HOW TO STUDY THE BIBLE

1) Be in an attitude of prayer. It's important to pray before, during and after the time of Bible study. Let your attitude be, "Lord, open my eyes to your truth and teach me."

2) Be consciously controlled by the Holy Spirit. It's the Holy Spirit who teaches and guides us. We need to rely on Him. If we don't, our time in the Word will be futile.

3) Be prepared for a rewarding time.

4) Be prepared for hard work.

5) Come fresh and alert.

6) Come expectantly.

7) Study it regularly and consistently.

8) Share with others what you've learned. Make it an active part of your conversation.

9) Be obedient.

## TOOLS TO HELP YOUR STUDY

Just as you need tools to build a house, so you need tools to effectively study the Bible to build God's Word in your life. Here are just a few that will be helpful.

1. A pen and paper. I've learned the importance of these simple tools the hard way. So many times God has revealed tremendous things to me as I read the Bible. I've thought, "I'll remember

that." But the inevitable always happens when I don't use a pen and paper. I would forget what I learned. Write down things God has taught you. Then you'll be able to review what you've learned. You might also want to highlight things in the Bible with a colored marker.

2. Webster's Collegiate Dictionary.

3. A Bible Dictionary (e.g., The New Bible Dictionary and Unger's Bible Dictionary). This gives great insights into words, people and places in the Bible.

4. A Bible Handbook (e.g., Unger's Bible Handbook and Haley's Bible Handbook). A helpful guide as you study the Bible! It gives good insights into various passages of Scripture.

5. Word study books (e.g., Vine's Expository Dictionary of New Testament Words). A must if you want to know detailed meanings of words in the Greek language.

6. A commentary or Study Bible (e.g., MacArthur Study Bible, ESV Study Bible). Tremendously valuable for studying books of the Bible. It gives outlines and explains what the author is saying line by line and verse by verse. It also gives good background material so you'll know the who, what and why of a book.

7. A concordance (e.g., Strong's Exhaustive Concordance and Cruden's Concordance). Beneficial for looking up brief definitions of words. It also gives many references in the Bible where a particular word is used.

8. Topical Bible (e.g., Nave's Topical Bible). Ideal for studying topics such as salvation, the Church, etc. It will list every place a topic is used in the Bible.

9. Study Guides. John MacArthur has some of the best I've seen on any book of the Bible. They take you through books, giving charts, questions, information and direction.

10. Audio messages. One of my favorite tools for studying. Downloadable sermons can be used to make wise use of your time as well as give you the opportunity to learn from Bible scholars. You can listen to them messages while driving, relaxing around the house, working, etc. One of the best free sermon downloadable sites is www.gty.org.

## METHODS TO HELP YOUR STUDY

There are numerous Bible study methods. Just as a carpenter needs tools to build a house, he also needs plans. We also need methods or plans for using these tools to get the most out of God's Word.

1. **Read.** You can read the Bible completely through in one year by reading three or four chapters a day. If you've never read it through, start with the Gospel of John and read through to the book of Revelation. After you've finished, start at Genesis and read through the Old Testament. Another way of reading the Bible is to read three chapters in the Old Testament and one in the New Testament each day.

**2. Topical study**

1) Select a Bible word in which you have an interest, such as God, sin, Bethlehem, etc.

2) Look up the word's definition in a Bible dictionary.

3) Using a concordance or Topical Bible, trace the word through the Bible. Much can be learned this way. For instance, the word "sin" means to miss the mark. It's used as a source of action Romans 3:9 and 5:12. It's also used as a governing power in our body in Romans 5:21.

4) Arrange the information in an outline form.

5) Make application from what you've learned.

   a) What impresses me?

   b) Where don't I measure up?

   c) What am I going to do about it?

**3. Book study**

1) Using a Bible dictionary, get the background of the book. Who wrote it? Why? When? To whom?

2) Read the whole book, such as Ephesians, through daily from beginning to end. Do this for four to six weeks.

3) Take a chapter a week, and as you read, use a Bible dictionary to look up key words and themes such as "choose," "adoption" and "predestined." These are key words in the first chapter of Ephesians. You might use Jensen's Self Study Guide or tapes. A Bible commentary would also help give good insight.

4) Re-read the book with this information in your mind.

5) Take what God has taught you and begin doing those things to make them true in your life.

**4. Character study**

1) Select a character in the Bible you would like to know more about.

2) Use a Bible dictionary for background information.

3) Using a concordance and cross references, study all the places the individual is mentioned. For example, John the Baptist was a preacher (Matthew 3:1), was direct in his approach (Matthew 3:7), and was a cousin of Jesus (Luke 1:36).

4) List what you feel are his strengths and what contributed to them.

5) List what you feel are his weaknesses and what contributed to them.

6) List the things you learned about this person and would like to see true in your own life.

7) Personal application.

Be creative in your thinking on how to study the Bible. These are only a few suggestions to help you get started. Also, it would be wise to read such books as *HOW TO GET THE MOST FROM GOD'S WORD* by John MacArthur and *HOW TEENS SHOULD READ THEIR BIBLES* by Joel Beeke for additional insights on how to study the Bible.

## APPLY WHAT YOU LEARN

Be obedient to what God asks you to do. When we fail to obey, our fellowship with God is broken. Ask God to reveal things that displease Him in your life. Then, diligently ask God to remove them. List specific things you need to do according to what the Bible has taught you. Sit down with a good friend and encourage one another—especially in touchy and sensitive areas (habits, weaknesses, etc.). Write in your schedule things you need to do in obedience to His word (e.g., witnessing time, memorization, a time to encourage, apologizing to those you've wronged, etc.)

The writer of Psalms 119:11 said, "Thy Word have I hid in my heart . . ." He did not say, "Thy Word have I hid in my notebook." Study and review what God teaches you as you use these Bible study methods. Study to know God's Word so that it becomes a living part of you. Study so that God's Word will accomplish, according to this psalm, it's purpose "that I might not sin against Thee."

# APPENDIX III

# HOW TO PRAY

## by Dan'l Hollis

The ultimate need of man is to fellowship with His Creator. Now that we're new creatures in Christ, we have the capacity (a spirit) to communicate with God, who is Spirit.

> "But an hour is coming and now is, when the true worshippers shall worship the Father in spirit and truth; for such people the Father seeks to be His worshippers. God is spirit; and those who worship Him must worship in spirit and truth."
>
> (John 4:23–24)

The above passage states that God actually seeks our worship and fellowship. That's amazing and hard to believe. God is self-sufficient, self-contained, in need of nothing, totally perfect and happy in and of Himself, and He actually desires our fellowship.

Fellowship is a two-way communication. God speaks to us primarily by His Word and we speak to Him through prayer. Since God looks for our fellowship in prayer, we should learn how to pray. May our attitude be that of the disciples, "Lord, teach us to pray" (Luke 11:1).

### WHAT IS PRAYER

Prayer is simply talking to God. It's coming directly into His very presence to fellowship and worship

God Almighty. In fact, Hebrews 4:16 tells us to "come boldly (with confidence) to the throne of grace." Boldly is a freedom or frankness of speech—the speaking of all one thinks. We are to be so open and free with God that we can talk about anything that comes to our mind. How wonderful to be able to be that free and open with the Almighty God of the universe. Most people think it would be tremendous to be in the presence of a king, celebrity, or superstar. Well, we can come before the King of kings and Lord of lords! Fantastic!

## THE COMPOSITION OF PRAYER

Prayer is made up of confession, praise or adoration, thanksgiving, petition and intercession. Let's look at each one to see what is involved.

*Confession* is God's designated means whereby we are able to stay in fellowship with Him. Isaiah 59:2 and Psalms 66:18 state if we have unconfessed sin in our lives we're separated from God and He doesn't hear our prayers. I John 1:9 gives us the how-to of regaining fellowship. Confess literally means to "agree with" or to "say the same thing." We agree that according to His standards what we have done is wrong. We name our sin, acknowledging what we did was wrong and thank Him that it's by the work of Christ we are forgiven (I John 1:7 and I John 2:2). We don't ask God to forgive us, but thank Him for having already forgiven us. Let's say you just lost your temper. You would say something like, "Father, I agree that losing my temper is a sin. I thank You that You have forgiven me because of what Christ has done. I want to be pleasing to You." One last point, sorrow is not part of confession, although it may accompany our confession.

*Praise* means to applaud or speak well of someone. It has the connotation of gratitude and thanksgiving.

God alone is worthy of our praise (Psalms 148:13). We praise Him for who He is—that is, His person and attributes—and for what He's done (Psalms 150:2). Our praise brings joy and pleasure to God (Psalms 147:1). All of His creation has been made to praise God (Psalms 148:1–6; 149:1; 150:6). This praise will flow from you when you're in His presence. For instance, after you've confessed, you may praise God for His grace (God's unmerited love). "Father, I praise you that I'm forgiven and now in fellowship with You again."

*Thanksgiving* means to be grateful and to give thanks for what God has done. Paul talks about this in his letter to the Thessalonians.

". . . give thanks *in all things* (good or bad) for this is God's will." So, we need to thank Him for what He's doing in our lives. You can thank Him that you're forgiven and that He's made a way for you to come back into fellowship. You can thank Him for the win or thank Him for the loss.

*Petition* is a thing asked for or something requested. Petition is simply asking God for your needs and wants. Here are some examples: 1) "Father, I want You to open my eyes to Your Word that I may understand." 2) "I pray that as I compete Christ will be seen in me." 3) Lord, I need a place to live."

*Intercession* is a technical term for approaching a king. Biblically, it means to seek the presence and hearing of God on behalf of others. This can be for material and physical things. You can say, "Lord, I pray for Bob. He's in need of Your peace right now as he goes through these difficult times."

Prayer is beautifully illustrated by the model prayer Jesus taught his disciples in Matthew 6:9–13. Christ didn't say, "Pray this prayer" or "Repeat after Me."

He said "in this manner pray." This is to be a model prayer. Christ not only listed the proper elements of prayer (confession, praise, etc.), but He gave insights into how our prayers may be effective and pleasing to the Father. The following is a list of His insights from Matthew 6:5–13.

## WHAT NOT TO DO IN PRAYER

1. Don't be as a hypocrite (verse 5). Hypocrites prayed long prayers trying to impress or inform people. Remember, prayer is direct communication with God alone.

2. Don't use vain repetition (verse 7). We're not to use meaningless phrases over and over in our prayers, such as, "Father," "Jesus," "Lord," "Thank you Jesus," etc. Even repeating Jesus' model prayer over each Sunday can be an example of vain repetition. God doesn't hear us for our many words, but because of what Christ has done for us.

This was brought home to me by my little two year old girl, Angela. I love for her to come and talk to me. But after the twenty-seventh "Daddy" I'm ready to climb the wall. God must feel the same way when His children wear out His name in vain repetition.

## WHAT TO DO IN PRAYER

1. "Go into your inner room" (verse 6). I believe Jesus is telling us to go into the depths of our soul. Having such an attitude, we can be open and honest with God and get down to the nitty gritty of life. In other words, lay your life open before God (Psalms 119:11, 139:23).

2. The phrase "and when you have shut the door" (verse 6) refers to spending time alone with God. You may be talking about things no one else knows

or should know. "Your Father who's in secret . . . sees in secret." He alone knows the secrets of your heart, your thoughts and motives, and every minute detail of your life. Be open and honest with Him.

> "And there is no creature hidden from His sight, but all things are open and laid bare to the eyes of Him with whom we have to do."
> (Hebrews 4:13)

## RESULTS OF PRAYER

1. The primary result of prayer is a response from God. God hears and answers our prayers (Jeremiah 33:3 and John 5:14–15).

2. Prayer enables us to resist temptation (Matthew 26:41).

3. Prayer renews our mind and spirit (Romans 12:2).

4. As we communicate with God in prayer, our fellowship with Him is strengthened.

## GOD ANSWERS PRAYER FOUR WAYS

God always answers the prayer of a person in fellowship with Him. God may choose to grant answers in four different ways:

1. Yes: The answer is in accordance with our request.

2. No. There are basically two reasons why we don't have results to our prayers.

A. We ask with sin in our life—wrong motives, attitudes, or actions.

B. God doesn't want this for us—it's not best. For example, I won't let my little girls play with a knife. I'll say "no" if they ask for one.

3. Wait. In other words, the best time is still future.
4. Yes, but the answer is in a different form than the request. For instance, we ask for patience and God gives us trials.

## FAITH IN PRAYER

An essential element in prayer is faith (believing God's Word). Faith is not persuading yourself that God will do it. Faith is simply believing God will do something because His word said it. Paul tells us, "Faith comes by hearing and hearing by the Word of God." (Romans 10:17). If God has not promised it, we cannot claim it by faith. We can claim by faith only that which God has specifically promised in His Word.

## THE PATTERN OF PRAYER

"For through Him we both have our access in one Spirit to the Father" (Ephesians 2:18). The object of our prayer is God, but there's a biblical pattern to be followed. The normal pattern is to the Father (Matthew 6:9), in the name of the Son (John 16:24), and in the power of the Holy Spirit (Jude 20).

## JESUS CHRIST IS OUR EXAMPLE

As you study the life of Christ, you find He was a man of prayer. If we are to represent Him as ambassadors (2 Corinthians 5:20), we need to see how He prayed and follow His example. Jesus began His public ministry and ended it in prayer (Luke 3:21 and 23:46). Throughout His life He continually spent time with His Father in prayer. He prayed alone and often (Mark 1:35; Luke 5:16). He prayed publicly (Matthew 11:25). He prayed when He was emotionally, physically and spiritually drained (Luke 5:15–16).

## THE PRIORITY OF PRAYER

Most of us feel when we're tired and exhausted, we need sleep. Yet, according to Luke 5:15–16, Jesus prayed when He was tired. Why? The spirit is what controls the physical and Jesus was always making sure He stayed in communion with His Father. He told Peter, "Keep praying that you might not enter into temptation, the spirit is willing but the flesh is weak" (Matthew 26:41). If Peter had kept praying he might not have denied Jesus.

One naturally thinks that Jesus would have slept the night before the crucifixion. He would have needed plenty of rest to have endured what He went through the next day. But no! Jesus thought it more important to pray. I feel we need to strengthen our spirit in prayer more than we need to strengthen our body by rest. I'm not saying that rest isn't essential. I'm saying that prayer is even more essential! It's my hope that your desire is that of the disciples. "Lord, teach me to pray."

## APPENDIX IV

# HOW TO WITNESS

**by Dan'l Hollis**

### THE BIBLICAL PREMISE

Jesus gives us one of the biblical premises for witnessing.

> "You did not choose Me, but I chose you, and appointed you, that you should go and bear fruit, and that your fruit should remain; that whatever you ask of the Father in My name, He may give to you" (John 15:16).

The word "choose" means to pick out for oneself. "Appointed" means to bring into a situation and to be put in the form of service. Christ has chosen and appointed us to the service of bearing fruit (witnessing).

Bearing fruit means we'll produce results. Quantity is not important—that's God's work. We're to pray and ask God to lead us to those who He has prepared. The fruit God has prepared (those who really believe in Christ) will remain (stay in God's family forever).

Jesus says, "abide in Me and my words abide in you" (John 15:7). Abiding in Christ (living and obeying His Word) is the life of fellowship with God, and the natural outflow is to share Christ. It will be as natural for us to share as it is for an apple tree to produce apples. "Apart from Me you can do nothing" (not one thing, not even one) (John 15:5). Christ living His life through us is the only hope for an effective outreach. If our vertical relationship is not right with God then we're bound to fail. Our outreach is what Christ does through us; it's a life style, not a method.

## WHAT IS A WITNESS

A witness is one who has information and knowledge on a subject and is willing to shed light on or confirm that which is under consideration. Jesus said, ". . . you shall be my witness . . ." (Acts 1:8). We are to share with others information we have concerning Christ—who He is and what He's done that they might come to know Him.

## WHAT DO WE SHARE

We share with men and women the Gospel, the good news concerning Christ. Paul states

> ". . . a bond-servant of Christ Jesus, called as an apostle, set apart for the *gospel of God,* concerning His Son, *who was born* of the seed of David according to the flesh, who was *declared with power to be the Son of God by the resurrection* from the dead, according to the Spirit of holiness, Jesus Christ our Lord" (Romans 1:1–4).

We're to share the Person and work of Jesus Christ. We share:

1. He is God (John 1:1, 14).

2. His death on the cross paid our penalty for sin (2 Corinthians 5:21).

3. The Resurrection—He has risen and is now alive (Romans 10:9). This is a proclamation concerning Christ—true whether men believe it or not.

The Gospel in brief—"Christ died for sinners," "you're a sinner," "believe on the Lord Jesus Christ and be saved." (Refer to chapter 2. It tells what is involved in believing). The *More Than Winning* booklet (an evangelistic tract to present the claims of Christ) may be used to share your faith effectively. *(www.morethanwinning.org)*

## HOW TO SHARE

1. Be in fellowship with God—empowered by the Holy Spirit.

2. Be in an attitude of prayer.

3. Begin with those closest to you (friends, relatives).

4. Be yourself. Relax and enjoy the time.

5. Share in love (1 Peter 3:15). Be sensitive. Be aware of his needs; don't embarrass or pressure him.

6. Be brief; stick to the Gospel; don't get off on other subjects, use the *More Than Winning* booklet.

7. Practice with a friend using the *More Than Winning* booklet.

## WHEN TO SHARE

1. As a way of life.

2. Spontaneous.

3. Any time or place that time and circumstances will allow. Be sensitive to the leading of the Holy Spirit.

## THE MEANS

The Gospel (Bible) is the only means which God uses to save His own people. Paul tells us, "Faith comes by hearing and hearing by the Word of God" (Romans 10:17).

Witnessing is God's idea, not man's. He commanded it and we need to be obedient and share the good news of Christ.

It has been said by Dr. Bullinger, "The Gospel has lost none of its ancient power. It is needed today as it was when it was first preached, the power of God unto salvation. It needs no pity, no help and no handmaid. It can overcome all obstacles and break down all barriers. No human device need be tried to prepare the sinner to receive it, for if God has sent it, no power can hinder it. If He has not sent it, no power can make it effective."

## BEING A WITNESS INVOLVES AN AMBASSADOR

An ambassador has the ministry of reconciliation (to change from enmity to friendship in the relationship between God and man), that God was in Christ reconciling man to Himself because of what God had done in Christ. Christ was made sin that we might be made the righteousness of God in Him. On these grounds, we have the command now to share with men how to "be reconciled to God." In other words, since men are sinful and alienated from God, they are invited to be reconciled to God; that is, to change their attitude and accept the provision God has made through Christ so their sins may be removed and they themselves justified to God. As ambassadors, (2 Corinthians 5:20), it's our ministry to share this with the world.

An ambassador tells others about the One he represents. We are to share who Christ is and what He's done. We are to witness not only by our actions, but by our words. "You are our letter, written in our hearts, known and read by all men; being manifested that you are a letter of Christ, cared for by us, written not with ink, but with the Spirit of the living God, not on tablets of stone, but on tablets of human hearts" (2 Corinthians 3:2–3).

## THE GAME PLAN

1. List the people with whom you want to share.

2. Pray for them that God will be preparing their hearts for His purpose.

3. Schedule a time to spend with them.

4. Go in His power.

5. Expect results.

There are several excellent evangelistic tools to help you present Christ clearly to him. You can get one such tool, *More Than Winning,* through the Fellowship of Christian Athletes at www.fca.org.

## THINGS TO REMEMBER

1. Salvation is totally of God from beginning to end. Yet, God uses men. You are simply an instrument in the hand of God. Jesus didn't say, "Fish for me," but "Follow Me and I will make you fishers of men" (Matthew 4:19). It's God's work and it's God using men.

2. Leave the results to God. As we share Christ and His Word, we need to keep Isaiah 55:11 in mind. It says, "So shall My Word be which goes forth from

My mouth; It shall not return to Me empty, without accomplishing what I desire, and without succeeding in the matter for which I sent it" God's Word will accomplish God's work. The results are God's. It's His Word and His creation. Men will not always respond the way we think they should. This should relax us to know it's not our smooth method. It is God who draws men to Himself. "Not by might or power, but by My Spirit" (Zechariah 4:6). The results are God's! He takes His Word and does the work in the lives of people as He pleases. What a thrill to be used by God to see men and women come to know Christ personally. May our attitude be that of Isaiah, "Here I am, send me."

## APPENDIX V

# ATTITUDE CONDITIONERS

Your actions are a direct result of what you are thinking. Therefore, it is highly important that you have the right thoughts in your mind. A Spirit-controlled athletic performance is the result of a Spirit-controlled mind. The following list of Bible passages has been compiled to help you have God's perspective on the various topics. The topics are listed alphabetically for your convenience.

### ANGER

Job 5:2
Proverbs 15:18
Proverbs 22:24–25
Ephesians 4:26

### AUDIENCE

Colossians 3:23
Philippians 1:8
1 Thessalonians 2:4

### AUTHORITY

Romans 13:1–5
Titus 3:1
1 Peter 2:13–14
1 Thessalonians 5:12–13
Ephesians 5:21
Ephesians 6:5–6
Colossians 3:22

1 Timothy 6:1
Titus 2:9

## CIRCUMSTANCES

Philippians 1:12
Philippians 4:11–13
Colossians 2:2–3
Luke 9:62
Philippians 3:13–14
Philippians 2:14
2 Corinthians 12:9–10
Romans 12:2
Ephesians 5:20
1 Thessalanonians 5:16, 18
Psalms 103
Isaiah 40

## COMPARISONS

John 21:21–22
2 Corinthians 10:12–13

## CONTRACT NEGOTIATIONS

Matthew 25:14–30
Matthew 6:24–34
1 Timothy 6:10
Luke 3:14
Hebrews 13:5–6
1 Timothy 5:8
Acts 20:35
Romans 12:3
Philippians 4:6–7
Philippians 2:3–4

## DEPRESSION

1 Corinthians 15:58
Philippians 1:6

Philippians 2:13, 17–18
Isaiah 40

## DISOBEDIENCE

Ephesians 6:1
Colossians 3:22
Ephesians 5:6
Peter 2:8
Jeremiah 11:3
1 Peter 1:22
Romans 6:16, 19
2 Corinthians 10:5–6
Hebrews 5:8
1 Peter 1:2
2 Corinthians 2:9
Philippians 2:8
Titus 2:9

## FAILURES

1 Thessalonians 5:16–18
Isaiah 40
James 1

## FATIGUE

Isaiah 40:31

## FEAR

Psalms 55:5, 22
Proverbs 29:25
2 Timothy 1:7
Proverbs 14:26
Psalms 23:4
Psalms 32:8
1 Samuel 12:24

Psalms 56:3–4

## HATRED

Leviticus 19:17
Romans 7:14–25
1 John 4:20–21
Proverbs 17:17
Matthew 5:43–48

## ILLNESS

Romans 8:18

## INJURY

Philippians 4:13

## LEADERSHIP

Philippians 4:9
1 Thessalonians 1:6–7
1 Corinthians 11:1

### LOVE

John 15:13
John 15:17
2 Corinthians 5:14
Isaiah 38:17
1 John 3:16

### MONEY

Hebrews 13:5–6
Proverbs 23:4–5
Timothy 6:10
Luke 3:14
Acts 8:20

## MOTIVATION

Psalms 42:1–2
Timothy 1:7
Proverbs 6:6, 9
Proverbs 13:4
Proverbs 26:16
Galatians 5:22–23
1 Timothy 4:7–8

## OVER-CONFIDENCE

Micah 6:8
Matthew 23:12
James 4:6, 10, 14
Psalms 78:39
1 Peter 5:6
Proverbs 15:33
Proverbs 29:23
Philippians 2:3
Colossians 3:12
1 Peter 5:5

### PAIN

Ephesians 6:10

### PRIDE

Romans 12:3
2 Corinthians 10:17
Galatians 6:3
Proverbs 16:5, 18
Proverbs 8:13
Luke 14:11
Proverbs 29:23
Proverbs 11:2

## REVENGE

Romans 12:19
1 Thessalonians 5:15
Ezekiel 25:15–17

## RECOGNITION

2 Corinthians 10:18
Romans 12:3
Luke 17:18
John 5:44
Proverbs 27:2

## SELFISHNESS

Philippians 2:3–4
James 3:14, 16
Luke 15:13
Acts 4:32, 34–35
Acts 5:1–6

## STRATEGY

1 Corinthians 9:26
Hebrews 12:1–2
Philippians 3:13–14
Ephesians 6:10–20

## TEAM SPIRIT

2 Corinthians 1:3–4
Ephesians 4:2–3, 32
Philippians 2:3–4
Titus 3:2
1 Peter 2:17
1 Peter 4:9

## TEMPER

Proverbs 15:18
Proverbs 22:24–25
Galatians 5:22–23
1 Corinthians 9:25
Acts 24:25
Ephesians 4:29

### WANDERING MIND

Colossians 3:23
Romans 12:2
Philippians 3:19–20
Matthew 16:23
Romans 8:5–8

# NOTES